■

"FOR WHERE THE OLD THICK
LAURELS GROW, ALONG
THE THIN RED WALL,

YOU'LL FIND THE TOOL- AND
POTTING-SHEDS, WHICH ARE
THE HEART OF ALL ..."

Rudyard Kipling
*The Glory of the Garden*

# BUILDING GREAT SHEDS

...

# BUILDING GREAT SHEDS

...

# DANIELLE TRUSCOTT

### WITH ARCHITECTURAL DESIGNS, PLANS, AND RENDERINGS
### BY BARRY HAMEL

LARK BOOKS

TO SUE L'HOMMEDIEU, WITH THANKS
FOR HER TIMELY OBSESSION WITH SHEDS AND INSPIRING SENSE OF HUMOR

ART DIRECTION AND PRODUCTION: Dana Irwin
ILLUSTRATION: Bernie Wolf, Dana Irwin
ARCHITECTURAL PLANS AND RENDERINGS: Barry Hamel
PHOTOGRAPHER: Richard Babb
EDITORIAL ASSISTANT: Heather Smith
PRODUCTION ASSISTANT: Hannes Charen

**Library of Congress Cataloging-in-Publication Data**
Truscott, Danielle, 1965-
    Building great sheds : creative Ideas and easy instructions for simple
structures  /  by Danielle Truscott ; with architectural designs, plans,
and renderings by Barry Hamel. -- 1st ed.
      p.   cm.
    Includes index.
    ISBN 1-57990-119-0 (hardcover)
    1.  Sheds (Buildings)—Design and construction—Amateurs' manuals.
    2.  Garden structures—Design and Construction—Amateurs' manuals.
I.  Title.
TH4955.T78   1999
690' .89--dc21                      98-51428
                                              CIP

10 9 8 7 6 5 4 3 2 1

First Edition

Published by Lark Books
50 College St.
Asheville, NC 28801, US

© 1999, Lark Books

Distributed by Random House, Inc., in the United States, Canada, the United Kingdom, Europe, and Asia
Distributed in Australia by Capricorn Link (Australia) Pty Ltd.,     P.O. Box 6651, Baulkham Hills Business
Centre, NSW 2153, Australia
Distributed in New Zealand by Tandem Press Ltd., 2 Rugby Rd., Birkenhead, Auckland, New Zealand

*Printed in Hong Kong*

ISBN 1-57990-119-0

# CONTENTS

If the mention of a shed brings to mind a falling-down, beat-up lean-to, or a boring, homogenous prefab aluminum box, you're in for a surprise. While many of us need a place to store things or to do odd jobs in, the idea of plunking down a slightly embarrassing structure in the backyard we've worked hard to beautify can send us scuttling straight back into the overcrowded garage. Cinder-block storage units on the outskirts of town begin to look good—at least they won't clutter up the yard! But they hardly make for convenience, if what you seek is easy access to stored items—and they certainly can't provide space for gardening or other work, or leisure activities. There are a number of companies that make kits from which you can construct quite attractive sheds, pool cabanas, playhouses and their ilk. But, as with most things, the nice ones don't come cheap, and most of us don't have or want to part with a lot of money to spend on building a shed. So what to do?

With *Building Great Sheds*, we've offered architectural plans, easy how-to instructions, and step-by-step photography, so that anyone with some time and energy can build an attractive, func-

tional, enduring structure for storage, work, or recreation. Our unique Potting Shed, handsome gable-roofed Storage Shed, and 12 variations on their two basic shapes provide a spectrum of sheds in different styles serving different and often multiple functions. Instructions for the Potting Shed, with its traditional shed roof, are so simple that even a novice can build it; the Storage Shed is easily manageable by most do-it-yourselfers; and the variations offer building projects to accommodate a range of skills, from beginning to expert.

Along with information on the tools and materials you'll need to complete these sheds, and helpful tips for first-time builders, you'll find interesting suggestions on how to spruce up and personalize kit sheds, and transform them into lovely, fun, and unusual structures that can add a dash of elegance or whimsy to your landscape.

Take awhile to meander through the following pages, and be inspired by the myriad—and often unexpected!—forms that sheds can take. Find the shed that's right for you, buy your building or decorating materials, gather your tools, and you're on your way!

# CHAPTER ONE

# A BRIEF HISTORY OF SHEDS

S ince human beings began building, in cultures around the world, people have erected secondary structures to store all manner of goods and vehicles, to house creatures of all kinds, to accommodate many and diverse kinds of craft work, domestic chores, and various personal regimens.

*For centuries, people in many cultures have built small secondary structures for storage, work, and recreation. American writer and naturalist Henry David Thoreau's cabin, no bigger than most sheds today, gives inspiration as to the many activities a tiny building can accommodate with some imagination.*

There are as many words used to describe these structures as there are different cultures that build them. How sheds came to be called such in the English language is an interesting, if somewhat unclear, moment where the history of English and western architecture intertwine. The use of the noun "shed" to describe a backyard or annexed structure comes indirectly from the verb

**ALL ARE ARCHITECTS OF FATE,**

**WORKING IN THESE WALLS OF TIME;**

**SOME WITH MASSIVE DEEDS AND GREAT,**

**SOME WITH ORNAMENTS OF RHYME.**

Henry Wadsworth Longfellow
*The Builders*

"shed." A single-pitch roof, as is commonly found on outbuildings, is referred to as a *shed roof*, because it's designed to slough off, or shed water. (Some purists include only secondary structures with this type of roof in the true shed category.) Shed roofs are the grandchildren of *pent roofs*, low single-pitch roofs attached to the side of a house or barn. In the early settlement days of the United States, an addition with this type of roof was often made to a main house. Accordingly, small buildings separate from the house used for such purposes came to be known as sheds, despite varying rooflines (the double-pitched gable roof is, in fact, the oldest known type of roof used on "sheds" in the U.S.).

Interestingly, there is relatively little recorded history on such an age-old, global phenomenon, in part, perhaps, because sheds are, let's face it, not a very glamorous subject (although Marie Antoinette, who held court amidst "sheds" she commissioned for her faux shepherdess settlement at the Petit Trianon, might beg to differ!). Also, while some such outbuildings made of sturdier materials such as brick and stone (and sometimes logs) still exist, most original outbuildings have long ago been lost to the elements and passage of time.

Evidence of their existence is slim, and comes largely from appraisers' records, written personal accounts—even patches of worn ground, discolored soils, and the growth of differing vegetation. Open a few standard encyclopedias or like reference books, and "shed" entries toss up an exhaustive number of definitions and synonyms: lean-to, shack, cote, hutch, pen (sty!), woodshed, smokehouse, springhouse, corncrib, toolhouse, granary, summer kitchen, outdoor oven, icehouse, milkshed, boathouse, carriage house, teahouse, garden shed, smithy's quarters, woodshop, poolhouse, bathhouse, sauna, privy ... ! The category of sheds, in fact, includes all kinds of small structures auxiliary to a main dwelling which, like houses, have throughout history been made from innumerable natural and man-made materials. In both indigenous and pioneer settlements around the world, as families outgrew their primary dwellings, they often built and moved into larger structures, transforming their original homes to be used for domestic work or storage. In some cultures or regions, in different historic periods, an addition was built on to a main dwelling to accommodate domestic work or storage needs. Sometimes, particularly in heavily forested locales, it was easier to erect additional buildings that served specific functions—as spaces for cooking, curing

meat, "refrigeration," storing foodstuffs and tools and vehicles, sheltering livestock, and weaving, making furniture or pottery, and other types of craft work. Thirteenth-century woodsmen in eastern Finland and northern Russia, for example, converted former hunting shanties into saunas and storage sheds for rye as they established more permanent settlements. Some Native American tribes such as the Cherokee constructed "hothouses" from logs, grass, and mud, to warm themselves in winter. In North America and some African countries, as well as in some Mediterranean regions, outdoor ovens were commonly constructed to reduce fire risks in main dwellings, and to keep homes cool in sultry months. Early German settlers to Pennsylvania in the U.S. built dryhouses, to dry vegetables and fruit for later consumption. The Dogon People, tribal people from southern Mali in Africa, built individual granaries for each family to store its personal stock of the tribe's staple dietary grain. In the Caribbean, small sheds were built on sugar plantations to store sugar. A typical colonial settlement in the United States included, along with the main house, a kitchen-"shed," a smokehouse, a springhouse, a granary, and an outhouse (many also included a toolhouse, for both making and using tools). The English, not surprisingly, popularized the use of garden sheds, first as accessories to formal gardens, and later as almost standard structures on the grounds of even the most humble cottages.

With the advent of electricity and its modernizing brethren, many of the structures built to accommodate work and storage requirements were abandoned, as the functions and activities they served returned to the home. (Thoreau alone, perhaps, persevered throughout in his home which was nothing more than a shed!) Yet today, the tradition of sheds and their many-named siblings survives in the form of woodshops, tool and garden sheds, and storage sheds, pool cabanas, and the like, in backyards urban, suburban, and rural, across the globe.

*"Sheds" have many different forms and uses. Top: New York's Sonnenberg Gardens hosts an exact replica, built at the turn of the century, of a Japanese Teahouse in Kyoto. Bottom: This Cherokee hothouse in Cherokee, North Carolina, was used by Cherokee people as storage space year round, and sleeping quarters in cold weather.*

*Most wood outbuildings from days of yore have not survived time and the elements, but many historic sheds built from brick and other hardy materials have remained intact. Top: Twin brick bathhouses which once served as changing-rooms for Charles Kelley King's guests now flank the Mansfield, Ohio, Kingswood Center's formal garden, created when the existing pool was filled in. Bottom: This brick garden pavilion at Monticello, Thomas Jefferson's historic estate in Virginia, has been well preserved.*

# CHAPTER TWO

# CHOOSING AND PLANNING YOUR SHED

**M**ost of us probably won't be designing, choosing a design for, or building anything quite as ambitious as Frank Lloyd Wright's famous *Fallingwater* to serve our backyard gardening and storage needs, but the advice is nevertheless sound. A few Sunday drives through the countryside, spying other people's sheds set back in yards along gold-and-russet autumn back roads, or peeking through the leaves of spring's silver-green lanes, can send the most hard-nosed and sensible among us home with visions of our ideal shed.

A classic miniature saltbox, its clean lines gleaming with shingles freshly painted white, rising in a sunlit stand of pines. A piquant Victorian wonder tucked amidst fragrant, golden forsythia. A sturdy, cozy "room of one's own,"

*This gorgeous 10' X 10' garden house in Greer, South Carolina, is a daily retreat for owner and Master Gardener Micki Gannon, who uses it for preparing garden projects, propagating seeds and other potting work, making floral arrangements, and throwing fun tea parties for girls in the neighborhood.*

> "I NEVER DESIGN A BUILDING BEFORE I'VE SEEN THE SITE AND MET THE PEOPLE WHO WILL BE LIVING IN IT."
>
> - Frank Lloyd Wright

all burnished redwood planes and shining glass, gentle sunlight streaming through the panes to warm your shoulders and back as you sit at a worn, well-loved table, potting sweet-scented violets or pineapple sage, or adding the final brush-strokes to a watercolor whose completion was long overdue. A whimsical playhouse in bright yellows, reds, and blues, stencilled with favorite storybook characters, for the kids! A low, bright adobe wearing the desert sun's patina. Or a romantic mock-cottage in stone, with ivy and wisteria trailing and weaving its way up along intricate latticework ... cupolas and turrets, porches and hothouses, fabulous arched doorways and outrageous rooflines, French doors flanked by picturesque window boxes spilling pale roses, dance in our heads. It's easy to get carried away with wistful thinking, *fast.*

Sheds come in all shapes, sizes, and designs. Top left: This sweet 8' x 10' garden shed with latticed portico in Asheville, North Carolina, is used by owners Dr. Peter and Cathy Wallenborn for storage. Top right: Though small, this elegant little structure houses all the hand tools owner Riley Owens needs to maintain his formal garden. Bottom left: interior of architect James Stageberg's garden house at "Wind Whistle", his home in Wisconsin. Bottom right: open-air adobe shed with tin roof at Sol y Sombra private gardens in Santa Fe, New Mexico.

**P**erhaps, after realistic consideration, you'll decide that one of these structures (or some combination of the features they boast) which so delights the mind's eye is, in fact, just what you and your family want and need. But it's important to remember that building a solid, long-lasting shed is not unlike building a house. The scale is different, but the process and results are basically the same. It's a big project that will take time and money. Once completed, the shed will be a part of your life and landscape for years to come. Designing, or choosing a design for a structure that will suit your needs, taste, schedule of available time and energy for building, carpentry skills (or willingness to learn!), and pocketbook, is important; doing this thoughtfully and thoroughly before you start to build cuts down on potentially huge headaches and hassles later on. It's handy to bear in

*Left: lovely octagonal garden shed in Biltmore Forest, North Carolina, built by owner Kirk Symmes. Top: Ohio-based Irish builder and thatcher William Cahill custom designs romantic thatched garden houses and sheds like this one for his clients. Bottom: Overlooking its Beaver Island, Michigan, garden, this neat and cozy potting shed serves as "a room of one's own" for B.J. Wyckoff.*

mind that Frank Lloyd Wright also said, "An architect's most useful tools are an eraser at the drafting table, and a wrecking bar at the site." Paper, of course, is a lot cheaper than lumber, and the cost—both in dollars and aggravation—of dismantling a half-erected building is worth a thousand erasers, and certainly a good few hours of practical imagining. You're the builder for this project, and though you may not be the architect, you'll be choosing architectural designs. So it's a good bet to avoid the wrecking bar and make use of that eraser as much as possible before construction begins, by pulling a patient chair up to reality's drawing board.

*Top left: Award-winning gardener W.C. Justice transformed a 1900s Asheville, North Carolina garage into this attractive structure for storage and relaxation. Top right: Beauty need not be sacrificed to function, as this beautiful storage shed designed by Pennsylvania shed-builder Nellie Ahl shows. Bottom left: By adding a small porch to this good-looking potting shed, Jack Beam created a structure for work and fun for himself and wife Helga in Asheville, North Carolina.*

*Bottom right: Even the simplest shed can be striking, like this one in Ferry Beach, Maine.*

## WHAT WILL YOU USE YOUR SHED FOR?

There are several key things to think through when planning your shed, but the first question to ask yourself is, What purpose will it serve? The size and design of, and materials used to build your shed should address the present and projected needs of you and your family. As the focus of this book is garden sheds, this may seem like analysis overkill—a garden shed, after all, is a garden shed, right? But, whether the shed will serve as storage or potting space, a place for work or play, or some combination of these functions, considering the basic points that follow will help you choose the shed that will best suit your needs.

*Thinking through the items that will be housed in a storage shed and how you'll store them is a smart first step in choosing a shed design.*

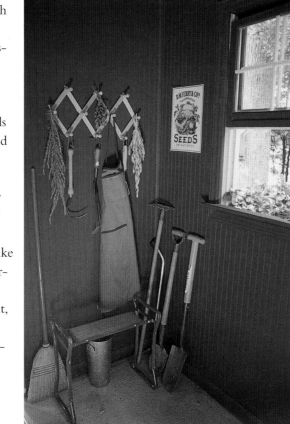

### THE BASIC STORAGE SHED

If your shed will be used solely for storage purposes, what will it store? You may need space for just an average array of the green-thumber's fundamental tools of the trade, such as rakes and shovels, bags of fertilizer and potting soil, weedwhacker, wheelbarrow, watering can, extra pots and stacks of seed packets, gloves, old sneakers, and other gardening gear. If so, anything from a simple, woodshed-style lean-to, to a basic 8' x 10' structure with an open entrance or single door may work just fine. Or will larger items make their home in this structure: a riding mower, a roto-tiller, even a small tractor? If so, how high and wide does the entryway need to be to accommodate larger pieces of equipment?

It also helps to think from the get-go about the interior space of your shed, about how you want to store the tools within, paying attention to creating easy access to those items used most frequently. Most of us lead busy lives. We want our leisure time to be—well, as *leisurely* as possible. If you're storing a riding mower in addition to lots of manual tools and pots, you won't want to have to move the mower every time you want to get to your shovel, or rake—or vice versa. A divided space, with one side housing the mower only, and the other accommodating other tools, may work best. How will you store those smaller tools? Hung on hooks, organized on shelves or in bins, or simply leaned and stacked in corners, or against the wall?

## Tips

*As you are thinking through what functions your shed will serve, make a prioritized list on paper. It's easy to leave "one little thing" out, which can cause problems later on.*

*Your tape measure is your best friend. No matter how good an eye for dimensions you have, it has a better one! Taking note of odd shapes or other qualities which might create storage dilemmas, measure the tools, pieces of equipment, tables, and other objects which will be stored or used in your shed.*

As always, it helps to think *way* ahead. Dreams of expanding your garden or transforming your landscape slowly over the years may mean you'll acquire more or bigger equipment in the future. If so, you'll want to plan your shed's size accordingly now. Even if you don't foresee adding much to your existing collection of trowels, hoes, and like gardening gadgets, it's not a bad idea to allow for a little more space than you think you need. As one Western North Carolina veteran gardener and shed owner put it, "Sometimes the gardening bug only nips you a bit in the beginning, but the itch has a way of growing and spreading so's you'd hardly notice, and it gets most of us full-blown in the end."

Like size and design, the materials you use to build even the most basic storage shed may depend in part on the tools and equipment it will house. Think carefully about the kinds of tools, equipment, and gardening accessories that will live in your shed, and consider: How weather-tight does the shed need to be? Will a little rust do little harm, or do the tools and equipment you plan to keep in the shed require complete protection from rain and other elements to stay in good working order? Does it matter if mice or other shelter-wily fauna make their ways in seeking winter nesting-nooks? Different foundations, kinds of lumber used for framing and/or siding, roofing materials, methods of joinery and other construction techniques—even types of nails—can make a big difference to the shelf life of stored contents.

### THE BASIC POTTING SHED

Most potting sheds, or sheds used for gardening work, also serve as storage sheds, even if the items stored are only a handful of small-scale potting implements that take up little room. And while the same considerations regarding size, design, and materials given a storage-only structure also apply to a potting shed, a shed used for "indoor" gardening work will require a bit more planning. With any luck, after all, you'll be spending some time in there! And even if the number of hours you imagine pleasantly whiling (or industriously perspiring) away in your potting shed are few, you'll want to make sure that the interior allows for a comfortably sized work

*Top and center: Even in a small shed, smart design means you can store hand tools and small equipment for gardening and have plenty of room left over for manoeuvering. Inset: Double doors make for easy storage of and access to larger items like riding mowers. Bottom: Inventive design elements such as this nifty fold-out potting shelf make optimal use of minimal space.*

17

space where you, your potting bench or table, an assortment of hand tools, and handy shelves for storing pots, plants, and bags of soil can happily coexist. If you're going to store many or large tools and/or

pieces of equipment in a shed where you'll also be working, make sure to allow enough room for them and you. In close quarters, bumping elbows with the often sharp and sometimes rusty angles of tools and machinery can take the fun out of recreation as fast as you can say *ow.* A dual-purpose shed need not be a big

shed, and simply assigning different uses to different interior areas, or building an interior dividing wall, may create appropriate space for both work and storage functions. Thoughtful, inventive design—for example, a potting table that lets you work inside or out, built as part of a wall and doubling as a window, as our how-to Potting Shed's does—can create in a small structure many of the spatial and functional advantages that only a large shed would seem to offer.

Once you've figured out the interior arrangement of space, there are a couple of crucial elements—namely air, water, and light!—that need to get in from the outside. Many potting sheds seem to do their duty and please their owners perfectly well without plumbing or electricity. In fact, a potting shed located close to the house or other outbuilding from which a hose can be run, with strategically placed doors and windows, can give you adequate light, cross-ventilation, and labor-minimizing access to water. If you live in a particularly hot or still climate, or envision spending long summer afternoons in your potting shed, you may want to install extra vents to make your time puttering among favorite flora more enjoyable.

*Top, center, and bottom: It's important to consider the size, design, and placement of windows and doors relative to specific gardening tasks that will take place in a potting shed.*

*A shed-sized building can serve many purposes. Top: A screened wall sides W.C. Justice's combination summer room, making it great for recreation as well as storage. Inset: A refinished wardrobe keeps old and unattractive tools and hoses out of sight. Center: This tiny log building makes a wonderful fine-weather playhouse for Dr. Peter and Cathy Wallenborn's daughters. Bottom left: In Charleston, South Carolina, this charming structure includes space to store pool and garden equipment, and an "upstairs" loft-style children's play area for T. Hunter McEaddy and family. Bottom right: Accompanied by a rear storage area, the enclosed porch fronting this unique building provides an area for relaxation, a cool drink, and a meal for its owners at the end of a long day's gardening work.*

## OTHER POSSIBILITIES AND FUTURE USE

Small, relatively inexpensive buildings such as those you will find throughout this book need serve not only as sheds for gardening tools and work, of course. The many styles shown in the how-to and inspirational sheds easily lend themselves to serving as storage places of all kinds, as well as small work-

shops, playhouses, back-yard mini-retreats, studios, "summer rooms," even (if your gardening talents lead to excess, and the entrepreneurial spirit takes hold of you) a plant or vegetable stand!

You may be looking for an affordable, attractive, good-sized storage option for pool equipment, to round up layabout pumps and filters, vacuum hoses snaking across walkways, and half-filled pails of chlorine and the like, that can turn the pool area into vaguely treacherous (not to mention unsightly) territory. A place to stack deck

chairs, tables, and umbrellas at the end of the day, or the end of the season—so they're still in good condition *next* season. If you're a handyman, or have one in the family, a garage whose dimensions once seemed nigh-on voluminous may now—courtesy of an ever-expanding stock of table saws and their kin—be a cramped series of Lilliputian labyrinths threatening even the car's sheltered spot. A spin down any highway in just about any locale, counting the numerous storage buildings for rent, shows that some of us just need more space for more ... well, more *stuff*.

As with a potting shed, if you plan on using your shed for recreation or work of some kind—as a summer "reading room," a place to draw, paint, or pen a patient Great American Novel (or a fun, safe place to send the kids while you do those things in the house!)—you'll need to think carefully about light and ventilation, possible plumbing and electricity requirements or how to circumvent them with appropriate design.

Again, far-sighted planning is a good bet. The Welsh poet Dylan Thomas composed much of his prolific and well-loved verse in a shed long used to store sacks of mulch and gardening tools, transformed into a "writing shack." Do you foresee using a small structure built now for other activities down the road? If you're building a playhouse for children, for example, what might you use the structure for when they are grown?

*Top: Perched beside a lily pond, this summerhouse-shed in Hudson, Ohio, makes a wonderful retreat for garden designer Valerie Strong. Center left: The interior of Strong's shed hosts an inviting sitting area. Center middle: This quaint pavilion nestled in the flora gives visitors a great place to stop and smell the azaleas at Maymont in Richmond, Virginia. Center right: You can't help but love the rural flavor of this shed (apparently a sometimes barbecue station and vegetable stand!) outside of Greenville, South Carolina. Bottom left: This lath-roofed shed provides partial shade and good air circulation for orchids raised by the Waltons in Ohio. Bottom right: Often, sheds built for one purpose find new life in later years—poet Thomas Rain Crowe stands in front of a garden shed wherein Dylan Thomas wrote many poems.*

*Building Great Sheds*

**O**nce you have worked through the practical side of planning your shed, you're ready to do the fun stuff. You know what the shed must do, and now you get to decide how it will look. Again, the verbose Mr. Wright's legendary maxim, "Form follows function," holds true. But for each set of functional requirements, there are myriad basic styles of architecture, interior and exterior features, and embellishments that will satisfy those requirements.

Today's market's extensive palette of types of siding, roofing materials, windows, doors, paint and stain colors, and hardware, makes your spectrum of style choices nearly infinite—and that can be a little overwhelming. The best place to start is to think about whether you want the shed to extend or complement the architecture and style of your house and/or other existing buildings on your property. If the hardware on the windows and doors of your house is made of brass in Colonial style, then modern, chrome hardware on your shed will disrupt the atmosphere you have created on your property. If your house has a gable roof, you may want to choose a shed design whose roofline will echo it.

Or maybe not. For many, one of the best things about building a shed is that it doesn't need to be taken quite as seriously as a house. You might not want to *live* in a scaled-down replica of the Taj Mahal, but why not have some fun with a building that is, after all, for recreation? Many shed-owners, in fact, think of their sheds as their property's

*The styles and finishes of sheds run from straightforward to wholly whimsical, sometimes matching and sometimes contrasting with other architecture on a property. Top left: This miniature Greek temple was designed and built by Stephen Pannell, whose company, Little Mansions, Ltd., concocts all manner of delightful, unusual playhouses and sheds. Top right: Sometimes round and bright is better, as illustrated by this delightful guest house. Center: This looks-good-anywhere garden storage shed, owned by Pat Schweitzer and Allen Vilcheck, is one of several the two have built for friends and clients. Bottom left: Materials recycled with superb imagination by John and Kathleen Holmes make their "Wizard of Oz" upside down garden shed in California truly one of a kind. Bottom right: A small, pastel A-frame shed looks wonderful tucked back in the trees and dappled by sun.*

*Artist Bob Comings' super-personalized garden shed in California has metamorphosed (and continues to metamorphose!) over time, as he covers it with wonderful found objects and other good stuff for an interesting effect.*

*This lean-to made of green lumber is typical of all-purpose sheds in rural areas.*

"conversation pieces." Radically different styles of architecture set in close proximity can be visually jarring, and can sometimes negatively affect your property values later on. But if you are staying put for a while and have enough land to work with, it can be fun to create the feeling of a different, separate environment within the property as a whole.

■

### WHAT'S THE BEST SITE FOR YOUR SHED?

Both in terms of appearance and function, location is a big factor in determining how your shed will best serve your daily activities. The most important things to consider are a potential site's levelness of ground, soil conditions, and the shed's relation to other structures on the property if built on that site. Level ground is optimum for building on, and site preparation—bulldozing a patch of land, removing trees and large rocks, etc.—is labor-intensive and can get expensive fast, whether you do the work or the contractor does. If you can build on soil that is naturally well drained, you'll save the cost and effort of installing an additional drainage system. Likewise, siting a potting or work shed to ensure easy access to water and electricity saves having to plumb and wire the structure. If hoses and extension cords must get from the house to the shed, make sure they won't lay across a frequently used driveway. More important, if you, your friends, or especially your children will be using the shed frequently, make sure that there's a path from the house to the shed that is driveway-free.

Views from and of the shed, the surrounding area's landscaping possibilities, existing vegetation on or overhanging a potential site, and orientation to sun and prevailing winds, should also be considered when choosing the ideal spot for your shed. When contemplating a possible site, think about its qualities in all seasons. If you're looking at the site in early spring, and the dainty leaves and buds on branches swaying above the roof charm the eye, think about those same branches in mid-January. You may not want to part with those branches, but years of snow-heavy or ice-wrapped branches thudding on even the sturdiest of roofs can cause disrepair. Similarly, if

*Choosing a site that is level and clear is, if possible, the best option for building a shed, since it means minimal labor and expense for site excavation and preparation.*

it's winter and your yard's densest vegetation is in hibernation, think about the plants, shrubs, and other types of vegetation that will poke their heads up in spring, and flesh out in summer. Will The Return of Indigenous Vegetation conquer the shed? Will you have to cut down plants you'd just as soon leave where they are?

Often, a well-planned shed can improve the overall appearance of your property while incorporating native and existing trees, shrubs, and plants into the landscape. Think about how you might want to cultivate the landscape immediately surrounding the shed, too. Lots of shed-owners pave flagstone or other kinds of pathways leading to and from the shed, to minimize wear and tear from wheelbarrows

and mowers on the earth. In order to do this, the ground at the shed's front should be relatively level, and the soil should be easy to work with. If you want to plant particular flowers or shrubs around, in front of, or leading up to the building, will they get enough sun in this location? Will prevailing winds knock your sunflowers on their backsides?

First things first, of course. Likely as not, no prevailing winds will knock you on your backside if you're working (or playing) inside the shed, but you don't need them proudly flouncing through open windows and doors delivering unpleasant draughts down your shirt as you're just settling in to relax with a flat of new begonias. Conversely, if you live in a particularly hot climate, or plan on spending a lot of time in your shed in the summer months, perhaps a little excess ventilation is just what you need.

At the same time, if you plan on spending time in the shed, think carefully through how the shed sits on the site in relation to sunrise and sunset, to assure optimum light while you're potting, writing, composing music, painting, or carrying out other tasks. You may want to think about the view from inside, too. If you'll be using the structure for potting work or artistic endeavors, a visible mountainscape, entrée on to a forest, desert panorama, or rolling pasture topped by blue sky and fantastically shaped clouds can be all the inspiration or muse you need. What about views of the shed from other vantage points? Do you want it to be visible from your house, from your neighbors' houses, to passersby? If you're storing valuable equipment in the shed, a more secluded, secure location may be preferable. If it's a recreational shed, do you mind if someone stops in to say hello? Or would you prefer a little privacy, nestled away behind a row of trees, or in a back corner of the property, where privacy, peace,

### Tips

*If you're not in a hurry to start building, photograph potential sites in different seasons. Photocopy pictures of sheds and paste them in!*

*As you are considering different sites, bear in mind that selecting a location where the ground is already*

and quiet can reign? Since breathtaking, or just plain old favorite views are things most of us hold dear to our hearts, instinct will probably ensure that you don't build the shed so that it blocks a best-loved vista from your own home. In the interest of community relations and the sure future of borrowed cups of sugar, though, you may want to take your instinct over to your surrounding neighbor's yard, and make sure the shed won't block his, her, or their treasured view if placed in your chosen site.

Ultimately, the old saying "You can please some of the people all of the time, and all of the people some of the time" wins out, with this twist. Replace "people" with "conditions," and you may find yourself at the mercy of the maxim when siting your shed. You may not have an absolutely ideal spot that addresses all of your needs and wants. If that's the case, go back, prioritize your list and see what you don't mind doing without. Whether your guiding principle is beauty, practicality, environment, or—let's face it—budget, you'll most likely be able to make a few compromises that solve the problem.

# What About Building Codes and Permits, Zoning Ordinances, And Other Legal Stuff?

Of course, decisions made on the size, design, style, and siting of your shed are not entirely in your hands. Whether you see it as a blessing (Hurrah! You lose some responsibility!) or a curse (Aaaah! You lose some control!), your area's local building codes and zoning ordinances have the final say on where your shed goes, how big or small it is, what it looks like, and even, in fact, whether you may legally build a shed on your property at all.

There are almost no areas left in the United States that allow land use with no zoning restrictions. Building codes and permit requirements vary from state to state, region to region, municipality to municipality, rural area to rural area, even "backwoods" to "backwoods," and the only way to find out exactly what permit you need or don't need is to call your local building inspector and ask that person directly. Guessing at what you can or can't get away with is a dicey *modus operandi*, as can be relying on friendly, well-intended neighbors' advice that officials "don't really bother about enforcing" codes and regulations.

It's true that in most very rural areas, there is no need to obtain a permit for a shed, as it is considered an accessory building. In short (as long as the shed doesn't become an accessory to any crimes or misdemeanors your neighbors might see fit to commit when a finished shed about which they have not been consulted offends them), you may be all right putting up just about any kind of shed you choose. Likewise, "temporary" sheds (sheds without foundations) built anywhere often don't— but sometimes do!—require a permit. It's also true that different communities enforce rules and regulations more and less stringently than others.

Most communities do require permits to build anything other than a temporary shed, however, and do enforce building codes and zoning regulations with regularity and tenacity. Simply put, building codes set standards for material use and construction techniques, to ensure the safety of structures built; zoning ordinances determine the heights of buildings, lot coverage, and can arbitrate architectural design standards. The two restrictions most strictly enforced across the board are size regulations and "setback regulations," which determine how far from the property line the shed must be sited. The 8' x 10' sheds we'll show you how to build in this book can be legally erected in most communities, as there are very few ordinances that prohibit structures under 10' x 12', assuming they comply with other codes and regulations. In some suburban and other densely populated areas, though, there may be restrictions even on 8' x 10' and smaller structures. If human beings or animals will inhabit the structure (and the definition of "habitation" can, but does not always, include recreational use), still different codes and regulations apply. Similarly, if you live in a development community or a historic neighborhood, you may be required to have your plans, proposed site, and building materials O.K.'d by your homeowners' or historic preservation committee. Additionally, some building departments require that pre- and post-construction surveys be done, to assist in annual tax assessments of your property. You may have to have your property surveyed with the proposed site, and an as-built survey upon the completion of construction.

Once you have made all the necessary inquiries and gathered any permits and other forms you need, fill out the forms and submit them to the appropriate agencies. Your permits should be approved within a month, and then you can start building your shed.

**M**ost basic garden sheds are not plumbed or wired, but if you build your shed far from the house or another plumbed outbuilding, you may want to install a simple hose bibb. If you plan to use the shed as an artist's studio or a summer "rec room" for the kids, however, it may make sense to put in a full sink. Fortunately, even the more fanatical gardeners among us tend to limit potting and other indoor gardening activities to daylight hours, and most artists prefer natural to artificial light. But if you plan to read, write, or draw in your shed, and the romance of working by candle-or oil-lamp-light is—well, not so romantic, a rudimentary lighting system (even a single bulb) may be in order.

If you are a seasoned backyard builder and do-it-yourselfer, you may well have already installed plumbing and/or wiring for other structures or projects. If not, don't feel daunted by the prospect. Elementary plumbing and electrical systems are pretty straightforward and logical, and there are a number of thorough, reader-friendly books on installing simple to complex systems for both amenities available in home improvement centers and bookstores. The first step is to consult your local building department officials, who will inform you of codes for plumbing and wiring, and inspect the work you have done before you finish interior walls, floor, and (if you are doing electrical work) ceiling. Some codes mandate that a licensed plumber or electrician do certain jobs, so unless you're lucky enough to have friends or relatives in the trades who owe you a favor or two, you may have to hire a contractor for some of the work. Witticisms about tradesmen making more money than white-collar folk don't rely entirely on fiction

> **Tips**
>
> *Don't buy any pipes, fittings, hoses, fuses, wiring, or other materials before you have researched local building codes.*

for their humor, and the punch line can be particularly unamusing when an astronomical bill makes you feel like the butt of the joke. In other words, carefully consider whether potential plumbing and electrical utilities are worth the expense their installation may rack up. Most important, if you choose to plumb and wire the shed yourself, pay close attention to safety procedures listed in whatever manual you use. Local building department officials may have safety guidelines and/or tips, or, ask a friend (or friend's friend) who is a licensed plumber or electrician for advice. Jokes involving poor plumbing systems combined with poor electrical systems are few and far between, and the safety of your structure and the people using it is paramount.

*Left: Most potting sheds do fine without plumbing or electricity, but a simple system for using hoses outdoors (left) and means of ventilation (right) and/or light can make for greater ease while working and playing inside and out of the shed.*

# How Much Time and Money Will It Take To Build Your Shed?

## Your Skills and Budget

The cost of building a shed can vary enormously depending on site preparation requirements, potential tool and equipment purchases, the shed's dimensions, types of materials used to build and finish it, and any amenities—plumbing or electricity, for example—with which you choose to outfit the shed. The sheds and building techniques offered in this book are designed to minimize costs for tools and materials, while still providing a wide range of handsome, durable, multiuse styles to choose from. If you own a basic "backyard carpenter's" tool kit, you won't have to purchase new tools, and any of the basic tools you may have to pick up are inexpensive. Similarly, the materials used for foundation, framing, roofing, and finish are all widely available and wallet-friendly; a fast, easy way to figure out your materials cost is to show your plans to a building supplier in your area, who will give you a free estimate.

Since you're building the shed, the only other cost is in your hours and energy. Your skills and the type and style of the shed you choose to build will, of course, determine in part how long it takes you to build it. Those who have tackled projects this size already will likely find building some of the sheds shown in this book easy, while some of the variations may provide fun, interesting challenges. We've provided instructions so simple and detailed for our classic Potting Shed that with a rudimentary knowledge of carpentry and willingness to proceed methodically anyone can build it. The same basic construction principles apply to all 12 of the sheds included in this book, so even a beginner with some diligence and time to spend can build some of the more complex variations.

Building anything that will last—even a step stool or birdhouse—takes time. It's awfully tempting, in the throes of inspiration, to think of a shed as a structure that's more closely related to a doghouse than an actual house. Hey, it's a lot smaller than Rome! Maybe it *can* be built in a day! In fact, a properly, thoroughly constructed shed probably won't be built in a weekend, or even two. And unless there is a particular and pressing reason to build the shed fast, you will likely enjoy the process (and keep many more friends) if you work on a timetable that is comfortable for you. For some, this means steady work over a series of weekends, or other free time; others may want to work on a more intermittent basis. Either way, if you work on a schedule that suits your temperament and available time in a realistic manner, you will likely find yourself making fewer mistakes, learning more, whistling rather than grimacing while you work, and building a better shed.

Moneywise, the best way to avoid any unpleasant surprises in later stages is to prepare a budget before construction begins. While there is no way to know exactly how much your shed will cost (as with all projects, in construction things have a way of changing a little along the way), you can start building your shed with a very accurate projection of your overall costs.

> ■ *Tip*
> Be realistic! Building a shed you can afford is far more satisfying than gazing woefully at a half-built shed you can't finish for love or money!

## Budget Checklist

| | |
|---|---|
| Excavation/site preparation | Tool purchases? |
| Footings/foundation (concrete) | Equipment rental? |
| Framing materials | Allowance for unforeseen expenses |
| Roofing materials | Plumbing |
| Siding and trim | Wiring |
| Windows and doors | Landscaping |

# CHAPTER THREE

# T O O L S ,   T I P S ,   A N D   S A F E T Y

T he idea of building a structure that is essentially a small version of a house can be overwhelming if your resumé of do-it-yourself woodworking or carpentry endeavors lists mostly small projects. Sure, you know how to measure, mark, and cut wood. You can bang nails—and pull them, when necessary. Your basic knowledge of geometry (those diehard remnants from high school or college courses) means you can translate simple spatial relationships into tangible, three-dimensional objects. But how to make the leap from building a bookcase or birdhouse to building ... well, a *building*?

In fact, these are the only skills you must have, or be willing to learn and hone, to build most of the sheds whose plans and elevations, materials lists, how-to instructions or general construction guides are provided in this book. We have kept the building techniques and directions so elementary that if you are familiar with hand tools and a couple of portable power tools (a drill, a circular saw, and a jigsaw) from the most rudimentary homeowner's kit, you're in good stead. And since the tools required to build these sheds are as simple as they come, even a relative novice—with some time, patience, and determination—can build a shed that will suit his or her needs.

None of these tools is exotic or hard to find; if you don't already own the hand or power tools suggested, they can be purchased at a comprehensive local hardware store, many department stores, or any home improvement center. If you are knowledgeable about tools (or know someone who is who doesn't mind a little weekend meandering), perusing stalls at good flea markets can be a fun way to turn up inexpensive, high-quality tools and equipment; your local shopping newspaper or guide can also be a great source. Even if you are an especially intermittent "do-it-yourselfer," all of these tools will find use again and again, and are relatively inexpensive, sound investments. If your budget is particularly slim, you may get lucky and find a friend or neighbor who doesn't mind lending you a posthole digger or jigsaw, and reduce expenses by borrowing.

It's common lore that woodworkers, carpenters, and even hobbyists guard their caches of tools like newborns. If you find one who's willing to lend you a power tool, write a book on your methods of persuasion! If you don't own or want to buy the couple of power tools you need to build the shed of your choice (or opt to use certain power tools instead of hand tools, to speed the construction process along), you may be able to rent them at a local rental business or lumberyard. Many rental businesses offer a wide array of power tools "for hire" by the hour or day. Make a realistic estimate of how long the job requiring a particular tool will take, though, and do the math before you rent. If you'll be renting a power tool for more than a day, it may be more economical to buy it.

This chapter lists and provides you with basic information on all the tools you need, or may opt to use, to complete construction for our Potting Shed and Storage Shed, along with some tips on use and maintenance for beginners. Construction for one or two of the more complex variations on these two basic designs requires additional tools, which are listed with the materials lists for individual sheds in the plans section at the back of the book. Below, you'll find information on power tools you'll need for those variations, too.

## HAND TOOLS

### CARPENTER'S PENCIL

Almost every step of the construction process requires you to mark dimensions once they have been measured. A carpenter's pencil, which is larger and more substantial than an average writing pencil, is the best implement to use for this purpose. The thick, dense lead tip of a carpenter's pencil won't break marking dense wood the way a finer point might, and can still be erased if necessary.

### FELT-TIPPED MARKER

Centering the six concrete piers that will serve as your shed's foundation requires using *batter boards*, a

temporary structure of 2 x 4s set up, along which a string (see *Mason's Line* below) is adjusted to find right angles and then marked. A felt-tipped marker will do the job nicely. Since you may need to readjust the string a few times and make several marks on a small area of string before you locate exact center points, it's a good idea to have a couple of markers in different colors, to avoid confusing different sets of marks.

### UTILITY KNIFE

This inexpensive tool is handy both for

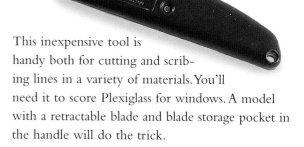

This inexpensive tool is handy both for cutting and scribing lines in a variety of materials. You'll need it to score Plexiglass for windows. A model with a retractable blade and blade storage pocket in the handle will do the trick.

### GLUE GUN (OPTIONAL)

You will need to apply a heavy-duty wood glue (see *Fasteners and Miscellaneous Materials*, Chapter Four) to the floor joists of your shed before laying the plywood floor. Wood glue comes both in squeeze bottles and in canisters which fit into a glue gun that works like a caulking gun; applying glue to the joists using a squeeze bottle will work just as well, but using a glue gun can ease and speed the process.

### MASON'S LINE

*Mason's Line* is just a carpenters' trade name for string. When finding the centers for your concrete piers, the string you use will be stretched taut, loosened, adjusted,

readjusted, and marked, so make sure that the string you use is easy to work with, and of a light color—preferably white—so that marks show up clearly.

### CHALK LINE

This little tool helps you to mark long, straight lines quickly and accurately. A small case with a reel-handle allows you to let out lengths of chalk-covered line. When you stretch this line taut between two points and snap it in the center, chalk dust from the line leaves a long clear mark between the two points. It will come in especially handy when marking multiple boards that must be cut to identical lengths or angles.

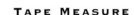

### TAPE MEASURE

The phrase, "Measure twice, cut once" isn't a hallmark of carpenters' wisdom for nothing. Accurate measuring and marking is perhaps the most crucial aspect of any construction project. A standard model tape measure with a 25' retractable steel tape will meet all the measuring needs for building your shed.

### 4' CARPENTER'S LEVEL

Throughout the process of building your shed, you will need to check both spatial and constructed surfaces to ensure that they are precisely horizontal. A standard 4' carpenter's level, also called a *spirit level*, will work best for this purpose. (If you already own a slightly smaller or larger level—a 3'

evel, for example—this will work fine.) To ensure level, place the 4' level on and flush with the surface you are checking. If the surface is level, the bubbles in the level's glass vial will be centered relative to marks on the vials.

### LINE LEVEL

Like a carpenter's level, a line level allows you to ensure that surfaces are precisely horizontal. Since a line level is small, light, and can be hooked on taut string, you will use it when working with batter boards and mason's line to find exact centers for your shed's concrete piers.

### PLUMB BOB

A plumb bob serves much the same purpose as a spirit or line level, but it works in a different plane, allowing you to ensure that spatial or constructed vertical spaces are precise. A plumb bob is a weighted line that works by gravity. If you attach the line-end of the plumb bob to a fixed point, or hold it directly above a point you wish to mark, the line falls to a second point exactly below the first.

### FRAMING SQUARE

This tool, which helps you test for squareness, is a must-have for laying your roof rafters and checking for the squareness of joints and corners. A framing square is simply a large square with two steel arms—one 24" long, and one 16"—joined at a right angle. It will also come in handy when you need to mark perfectly straight lines on boards.

### SPEED SQUARE

Like a framing square, a steel speed square is used to determine the squareness of joints and corners, to find angles, and as a guide for straightness when marking dimensions. Because it is so compact, a speed square is particularly handy when testing for square or determining angles in small spaces.

## RATCHET AND SOCKET

These little tools do the work of other types of wrenches more easily and quickly. You'll use one to fix lag bolts that secure hinges to doors and like elements, so a

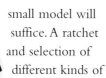

small model will suffice. A ratchet and selection of different kinds of sockets are good general tools to have around the house, and are sold in small kits for little expense. If you want to purchase only one socket, an adjustable socket, which allows you to turn and tighten bolts and other fasteners of all sizes, is probably the best way to go.

## CURVED-CLAW HAMMER

Since all of the nails you drive to construct your shed must be flush with the wood's surface, a bell-faced, 16-ounce curved-claw hammer is the best all-around tool to use. (This is also the best tool for pulling nails, which hopefully will account for a minimum of your hammering activities!) When purchasing a hammer, choose one with a well-finished, drop-forged steel head (rather than cast-iron, which chips and shatters more easi-

### "TOENAILING"

*Driving a nail at an angle to secure one board to another board is referred to as "toenailing." To toenail two boards together, hold the nail in place at a slight angle pointing down, and tap the nail's point in approximately $^1/8$". Then shift the nail head up to a 60° angle, and drive it into the wood. Nails driven close together using this method should be staggered, so they don't get in each other's way.*

ly). Hammer handles are made of hardwood, fiberglass, or steel, all of which will absorb shock in varying degrees. Driving nails accurately requires that you grip the handle lightly but firmly at its end and let the handle act as an extension of your arm, with the swing's momentum doing most of the work.

It is important that the handle is long enough to drive nails with the momentum of the swing, while still allowing you to control the swing's arc. While shopping for the right hammer, pick up hammers of different lengths, weights, and handle materials, and give them a swing or two to find which feels best for your hand and swing.

## CROSSCUT HANDSAW

All of the cuts necessary for framing, siding, trimming, and roofing your shed can be made with this simple hand tool (although using a circular saw for some cuts will make the process easier and faster), which consists of a wooden handle and a durable, low-mainte-nance stainless or tempered steel blade. Crosscut handsaws, which come in a range of blade lengths, have ten to 16 teeth per inch; the teeth are beveled to cut cleanly through boards, with a greater number of teeth giving a cleaner cut. When buying a crosscut saw, first test the blade in two ways: Tap it and make sure it gives a clear ring; then flex the blade, which should arc into a half-circle and bounce back into line when let go. A key to ensuring better cuts is to make sure the saw feels comfortable in your hand. Since a longer blade will accomplish the cut in fewer strokes, try out a few different lengths to see how long a blade you can manage. Crosscut saws cut on the push stroke, so make sure you can line up your sawing

shoulder over the work, letting your body weight do as much of the work as possible.

A well-maintained saw is easier, more accurate, and safer to use, and will slice through the wood with little effort. As soon as the teeth of your saw begin to dull (the blade will start to flex and wobble as it moves through the wood), have the blade professionally sharpened. To keep the sides of the blade supple, you can rub plain bar soap—or better yet, paste wax or paraffin—into the steel. You should also clean the blade from time to time with mineral spirits and steel wool. Last but not least, hang up your saw when it's not in use, so that the teeth don't get damaged.

### Posthole Digger

Depending on the soil conditions you are working with, you may be able to dig the holes for your foundation's concrete piers with a shovel. If you are working with difficult soil that is hard or rocky, you will certainly want to use a posthole digger, which will make excavating any type of soil much easier. Posthole diggers come in a couple of styles; here, your needs will be best met by a two-handled posthole digger with "clamshell" blades. If you don't own a posthole digger, but are planning to build fences as part of landscaping your property, it may serve you well to buy one. Otherwise, your best bet is to rent one from a local lumberyard—someone working there will also be able to show you how to use a posthole digger properly, if you haven't used one before. You can also rent a power auger, which does the same job in a fraction of the time.

### Square-Edged Shovel

A standard square-edged shovel will come in handy for any minor site excavations, digging holes for the concrete piers (if you choose not to use a posthole digger or power auger),

backfilling around the piers, mixing concrete, and post-construction landscaping.

### Screed

Like mason's line, *screed* is a fancy term for something utterly plain—a straight 2 x 4 used after you have poured concrete to remove excess in order to bring the surface to grade. The forms you are pouring concrete into are eight inches in diameter, so you'll want a 2 x 4 at least a foot long. Any old piece of lumber this size will work.

### Stepladder

Even many garages that don't belong to home handypersons include a stepladder, for general purposes like changing light bulbs just out of reach, entering attics, or cleaning high ceiling corners. If you own or have access to a sturdy, 10' stepladder, this will allow you to check levels for the tops plates and higher elevations in framing the walls of your shed, as well as providing safe, comfortable access to necessary roofing jobs. A higher stepladder will work just as well, providing it isn't so high that you have to *drop* to the roof, of course! Either way, the stepladder should have grooved treads (with angled metal braces on the lowest tread), and non-slip safety shoes. An extension ladder can be used, if that's what you have at hand, although it is likely to make for more awkward maneuvering when working on a relatively low roof. When using a ladder of any kind— particularly in combination with using tools— make sure its base is set firmly on the ground. An extension ladder should be securely placed against the wall, or the edge of the roof, where you are working.

## WHEELBARROW

A small amount of concrete, as is required for the foundation piers for your shed, can be mixed by hand on a large, flat surface like a concrete or cement driveway, covered with plastic, or in a variety of vessels. A wheelbarrow works best, as its mobility means you can mix the concrete only inches from where you need to pour it, and its shallow depth makes for easier mixing. Clean the wheelbarrow out as soon as possible after mixing and pouring the concrete, which, of course, hardens quickly.

## SAWHORSE

A solid, well-constructed sawhorse is an essential piece of equipment for any woodworking or building project that requires cutting long boards or large pieces of plywood, both of which you will be doing to frame and side your shed. If you don't own a sawhorse and are feeling especially energetic, you may want to build one yourself. Many comprehensive homeowner's do-it-yourself and basic woodworking manuals offer foolproof instructions. Otherwise, pick one up at your local home improvement center.

## WORK PLATFORM

In building your shed, you will frame the walls before you raise them. This requires a large, flat, level surface on which to place, arrange, and secure timbers and boards. Once you frame the base and build the floor of your shed, this structure will serve perfectly as a work platform for building and raising the walls. If you prefer to spread out while you are working, you may want to set up a similar platform close to the shed site—the built walls will be heavy and raising them (especially if you are working alone) can be awkward if you have to haul them even a small distance.

## POWER TOOLS

Experienced woodworkers and weekend carpenters may choose to substitute some of the suggested hand tools with appropriate power tools. If you opt to use the suggested hand tools, you will also need to use three hand-held power tools—a drill. a jigsaw, and a circular saw—to complete some tasks, so make sure you have access to a source of electricity and extension cords if necessary.

## DRILL

You will use mostly nails as fasteners when you frame and side your shed, but will need a drill to drive screws for various other tasks. If you don't own any power tools, buying a drill is a good place to start; a drill fitted with different bits and attachments can not only bore holes (in almost any material) and drive and remove screws, but also grind, sand, and polish surfaces, along with many other jobs. A good overall drill is a standard ⅜" reversible variable-speed electric model, which can be fitted with a wide range of standard and specialized bits and attachments to

electric model, which can be fitted with a wide range of standard and specialized bits and attachments to accomplish many different tasks. For the jobs your shed's construction will require, a standard twist bit, which can drill holes up to an inch in diameter in wood, metal, and most plastics, will work well.

■

### JIGSAW

A hand-held jigsaw is used to cut curves and shapes in panels or boards up to 1-½" thick; it will come in useful when cutting out spaces in plywood for windows and vents in your shed's walls. A jigsaw's cutting action comes from a long, thin reciprocating blade that completes about 3,000 strokes a minute. A shoe that surrounds the blade can be tilted 45 degrees to the right and left of perpendicular. If possible, choose a jigsaw with variable speed control and orbital blade action, which moves the blade's cutting edge back and forth through the work during the blade's up-and-down cycle.

■

### CIRCULAR SAW

For cutting larger and multiple boards for framing and roofing and plywood siding— particularly for making angled or beveled cuts—a  portable circular saw will reduce your time and labor, as well as giving a cleaner cut. Simply put, a circular saw is a motor inside a handle-equipped case which powers a circular blade. Circular saws vary in size, which is determined by the size of the blade driven. While blade sizes can range from 3⅜" to 16⁵⁄₁₆", the most common and practical size is a 7¼"

model, which will serve the wood cut requirements of these construction projects nicely. Also, circular saws can make straight cuts in just about any material; if you choose to build our how-to Potting Shed, or a variation with a metal roof, the circular saw will allow you to cut metal roofing material if a supplier in your area can't provide it cut exactly to size.

When you use a circular saw, establish a secure footing, and let your upper body, shoulder, wrist, and hand guide and stabilize the saw as the piece of lumber you are cutting glides through the blade. Always set the blade to the depth the job at hand requires, as leaving the blade at its full depth regardless of the depth of a cut can result in *kickback*, a sudden pushing back of the saw toward the operator. (It's a good idea to stand slightly to the side while you are sawing in case kickback occurs.) Get and maintain a firm grip on the saw, starting before the blade enters the material you are cutting, and guide the saw straight along the cut line. When you are finished cutting, hold the saw firmly so that it doesnt' drop, and wait for the blade to stop before lifting the saw away from the work.

Any circular saw can be fitted with a number of different types of blades specialized for different cutting jobs. To build your shed, you will need a carbide-tipped crosscut blade for most wood cuts, a finer-toothed, all-steel blade for cutting plywood, and a special abrasive blade to cut metal roofing.

## ADDITIONAL POWER TOOLS FOR VARIATIONS

■

### MITER SAW

A miter saw, commonly referred to as a "chop saw" or "miter power box," is used to make multiple angled cuts for joints of door frames, moldings, and other more delicate architectural elements. Simply put, a miter saw is a circular saw set on a low metal stand. The stand supports a round table which rotates to different angles with the turn of the saw's blade. The saw can be set for any angle between 45 and 90 degrees, allowing you to make serial cuts without resetting. Like circular saws, miter saws come in a range of sizes; the most versatile size holds a 10" blade, and this will work well for the angled cuts necessary for the sheds offered as variations in this book. Likewise, miter saws can be fitted with a number of different types of blades: a combination blade will work fine; for especially fine cuts, use a carbide-tipped blade or a planer blade, which will give a smoother, cleaner cut. When you're using a miter saw, make sure it's bolted or clamped down firmly to your worktable or surface. Be sure to closely observe the manufacturer's instruction manual and safety precautions.

## ANGLED AND BEVELED CUTS

*An angled cut is a diagonal cut made across the face of a board; a diagonal cut made across the edge of a board is called a beveled cut. Making an angled cut with your circular saw is much like making a crosscut, or straight cut, but you will move your arm to the appropriate angle and guide the saw firmly from that position. To make a beveled cut, you will need to tilt the saw's blade and motor to the necessary angle, and then proceed as for a straight or angled cut.*

■

## TABLE SAW

Most likely, this tool isn't one a fledgling woodworker will have sitting around in the garage, and for good reason. A table saw, commonly called a "bench saw," is a relatively large and stationary piece of equipment, not among the least expensive power tools around, and can be very dangerous if used without sufficient operating know-how. Anyone using a table saw should proceed with great caution. If you are not accustomed to operating a table saw and choose to build one of the variations requiring its use, get a friend or neighbor to assist you with the cutting jobs involving the table saw. (Here's an opportune time to borrow the tool and reduce your labor while you're at it!)

Basically, a table saw is a fixed, inflexible table beneath which a motor-driven circular blade, which sticks out from a slot to cut work passed over it, is mounted. A miter gauge and removable rip fence align the wood or other material you are cutting. Generally, table saws are used to crosscut wide panels and rip long boards with extreme precision. Since many of the variations we've offered (see Chapters Five and Six ) specify board and batten siding, the table saw is required mainly to cut wood strips to make battens. In most areas, local lumberyards can do this work for you at relatively low cost, which is an option to consider if you don't already own a table saw. If you don't foresee it getting much future use, you'll probably save money by paying someone to cut battens for you.

■

## POWER TOOL MAINTENANCE

If you use your drill and power saws properly and keep them clean, neither will require much more maintenance—the best thing you can do to keep them in good working order is to follow the manufacturer's recommendations. To clean your drill, circular saw, or jigsaw, unplug it, and wipe it with a rag or sponge that's damp (not dripping) with water. It's also important to replace blades and bits that are damaged or worn out, sharpen them when dull, and store them where water can't damage them.

Keeping the baseplate of your circular saw clean with a damp cloth will ensure accurate, clean cuts. If the base plate is metal, you can use lacquer thinner to remove dirt, gum, or pitch; mineral spirits will work better for a plastic base plate. It's also smart to coat the base plate from time to time with paste floor wax to keep it cutting smoothly.

# SAFETY WITH TOOLS

Construction sites, even small ones in your own backyard, can be dangerous places. When using any tool, it's important to follow both the safety precautions provided in that tool's instruction manual and general safety guidelines.

If you are using a tool you have never used before, or have only used once or twice, familiarize yourself with its workings before you start to build your shed. Even a hammer or handsaw can cause serious injury if used carelessly or in a hurry, so before you begin a job, carefully think through why and how you will be using a particular tool. Try to foresee potential accidents, and take precautions. Power tools, of course, can be extremely dangerous, and should always be used with caution. Never use power tools around water or in damp conditions, or leave them running when you are not handling them; unplug them when they are not in use. Make sure that cords are well out of the way when you are cutting, boring holes, or driving screws, and that all cords and outlets are grounded. If you need to change a blade in your jigsaw or circular saw, or adjust a drill bit, unplug the tool before you make the adjustment or switch. If you are using the circular saw, make sure the safety guard is securely in place, and use a *push stick*—a block of wood will do—to guide the piece of lumber or other material you are cutting past the blade.

What you wear while you are working can keep you safe, too. Leave loose and billowy clothing, and jewelry that hangs or dangles, in the wardrobe. Wear sturdy work boots or shoes (steel-toed, if you have them); leather, or leather-reinforced cotton work gloves; close-fitting pants; and a short-sleeved shirt, or long sleeves rolled up past your elbows. If you have long hair, keep it tied back and out of the way. Safety goggles are a good idea, and a must when cutting metal. If loud noise or dust bothers you, be sure to wear earplugs that muffle but don't cut out sound, and wear a dust mask or respirator.

Lastly, work when you are well rested and have both the energy and time to work on the project. If you've had a rough day at work, or are tired or upset, don't head out to work on your shed with hopes of being distracted from other concerns. Frustration and fatigue can cause accidents even when all other safety standards are met. Whenever you are working, make sure someone nearby knows, in case an accident does occur and you need help.

# CHAPTER FOUR

# MATERIALS AND FINISHES

Like houses and other structures, sheds come in all shapes and sizes, and can be built from a wide range of materials, using many different types of construction and techniques. Take a shed-tour of the United States alone, and you'll find sheds made from cedar and redwood, pine and oak, locust and cypress, in a broad variety of framing and siding styles. Sheds both elegant and whimsical built from recycled lumber, metal, and other salvaged materials. Shiny aluminum sheds, plain-as-punch cinder-block sheds, stately brick sheds, historic sheds rising up in layers of stacked stone. Tipi sheds, made from tree trunks and canvas. Sheds constructed from tires packed with dirt, straw-bale and adobe sheds, igloo sheds made of ice, and sheds made of sod. Likewise, types of siding run the gamut from traditional wood styles—shingles, board and batten, scab board, clapboard, shiplap, textured plywood, and the like—to corrugated aluminum and galvanized steel, tar paper, plastic, snap-on canvas, and lattice trailing wisteria and ivy.

*Both the interiors and exteriors of sheds can be finished in many ways. This interesting roof construction painted in bright rainbow hues creates a child-delighting, visually enticing interior in one of Tony Nissen's "Once Upon A Time" playhouses.*

From foundations to roofs, sheds are built from many different types of materials. *Opposite:* Thomas Rain Crowe's two-story, octagonal "springhouse" in North Carolina's Smoky Mountains is constructed of locally milled fir and spruce supported by tarred and graveled piers anchored in a spring. *Top:* shed made from adobe at the San Antonio Botanical Gardens in Texas. *Bottom:* greenhouse shed with glass half-walls and roof in Clinton, Ohio.

There are sheds with gable roofs, shed roofs, gambrel roofs. Roofs made of wood shakes and shingles, rolled and shingled asphalt roofs, tiled roofs, metal roofs, thatched roofs, sod roofs, trellis roofs, glass roofs, sheds with solar panels in the roof! Types of windows and doors vary from double-hung to casement to fixed windows fitted with plate glass, Plexiglass, and stained glass, from typical shed doors made of shiplapped or tongue-and-groove boards or plywood, to more complicated Dutch, French, or sliding glass doors. Hardware selections run the gamut from the simplest hinge the local five-and-ten has to offer, to antique doorknobs and reproduction historic sliding bolts. Decorative embellishments abound, with cupolas and weather vanes a favorite among shed-owners from Maine to New Mexico, South Carolina to San Francisco. Underneath it all, what holds the sheds up varies too: There are lovely old sheds with stone foundations calling up the romance of the English moors, sheds on low wood

*Top left: Construction with rough-sawn lumber can be beautiful if done well. Inset: A traditional stacked stone foundation isn't a job for the faint of heart, but looks great! Top right: Roofs made of tin or other metals are typical on sheds, since they're inexpensive and durable. Bottom left: This wonderful little shed in rural Norway is made of sod and raw*

*birch, with a sod-and-grass roof. Inset: Do your gardening on the roof! Bottom right: shed made of redwood at Tucson Botanical Gardens in Arizona. Inset: Windows hand-painted with botanical motifs add an atmospheric touch.*

Top: This large concrete structure was originally built as a garage, but now serves as the garden "shed" at Wave Hill Gardens in the Bronx, New York. Bottom: The ancient art of thatching roofs belongs in the hands of experts like William Cahill, who added thatch to this shed's original shingled roof.

Top: Sheds built of brick like this old Ohio springhouse stand up well to time. Center above: Though stone is somewhat unwieldy to work with, sheds constructed of stone can look great, cost little, and last long. Center below and bottom left: Builder Tony Nissen, whose company "Once Upon A Time" creates marvelous playhouses for children, often combines many building materials in interesting ways. Bottom right: This shed at the San Antonio Botanical Gardens in Texas is made of plant stalks, with a roof of palm fronds.

stilts by the sea, sheds built on concrete blocks, piers, or slabs, and sheds with temporary foundations of rocks or concrete half-blocks.

In short, if you are an experienced, highly skilled woodworker or carpenter (or are particularly adventurous in tackling new building approaches), you may opt to use the plans we've provided for these sheds, substituting favored or intriguing construction methods or best-loved materials to achieve different looks, textures, or even functions.

To keep these projects economical, and easy enough that even those with a modicum of carpentry know-how can build them, we've chosen materials that will be widely available in any area, are long-lasting and relatively inexpensive, yet still good-looking and easy to work with.

The plans, instructions, and photos or illustrations for each shed are accompanied by specific materials and cut lists. Meanwhile, though, here is some general information on choosing, buying, and using different kinds of materials you'll need to build your shed from the ground up.

**A**ll types of building materials have their allures, but there is nothing quite like the smell of wood, new or weathered. So we've chosen different woods—pine, spruce, cedar, and plywood—as the primary building materials for our Potting Shed, Storage Shed, and the sheds that are variations on these two basic designs. To simplify the process for newcomers to the backyard building milieu, all the sheds are designed to be built from dimension lumber (standard-size boards and timbers such as 2 x 4s and 4 x 6s) and plywood sheets, with minimal cutting requirements. In other words, there aren't any tricks to buying the lumber you need. If you use the specific materials we've suggested, simply go to any lumberyard or building supplier, and give the salesperson a list. Salespeople at lumberyards and home improvement centers are generally very knowledgeable and helpful, and will answer any questions and advise you with any materials substitutions you might opt for. It's helpful to know a little about the kind of wood you are working with before you start, though, so here are some guidelines and tips.

■

## TYPES OF LUMBER

With some creativity and expertise, any kind of lumber can be used to build a shed. Some of the inspirational sheds in this book, built by their owners, were constructed from salvaged lumber. Apart from the obvious ecological and financial advantages of using recycled lumber, the process of finding and piecemealing "secondhand" wood for a construction project can be fun, challenging, and highly rewarding if you have the requisite knowledge about the properties of different kinds of wood. Yet even thorough knowledge of this type can't always outsmart the fact that using pieces of salvaged lumber whose sizes and strengths are not uniform can ultimately cause structural problems that detract from the longevity and integrity of your shed.

■

## HARDWOODS AND SOFTWOODS

Typically, lumber from common hardwoods and softwoods is used to build sheds. Softwoods are trees that grow quickly and are *coniferous,* or bear cones: pine, spruce, cedar, fir, hemlock, and redwood are softwoods commonly used in building, particularly for structural framing, flooring, and siding. Relatively lightweight and economical, softwoods are easy to work with. Hardwoods are trees that grow more slowly and are *deciduous*, losing their leaves every year—oak, birch, walnut, cherry, mahogany, and walnut are a few. Lumber from hardwoods is denser, heavier, and harder than lumber from softwoods; while hardwoods such as cedar, redwood, locust, and cypress are the most decay-resistant woods, they can also be somewhat more difficult for fledgling carpenters to cut and nail, and are generally more expensive than softwoods. Softwoods are cheaper and easier to find than most hardwoods, and are still dependably decay-resistant, so we have suggested using a combination of economical construction pine, spruce, and cedar for framing and trimming your shed and decking its roof.

■

## NATIVE, KILN-DRIED, AND PRESSURE-TREATED LUMBER

Both hardwoods and softwoods can be purchased in an unseasoned, seasoned, or treated state; lumber can be purchased in its native state, kiln-dried, or pressure-treated with preservatives which ensure protection against damage from rot, decay, and insects.

Native lumber, also known as "green lumber," has

been rough-sawn to rough dimensions at a sawmill. While green lumber can cost half as much as kiln-dried lumber, using it poses a real disadvantage for new builders; since it is not planed or dried, it is wet and heavy, and therefore can be hard to work with. You may be using this book just to get ideas and inspiration for your shed, and plan on building a rough-textured, rustic shed. If you are well versed in working with wood and working on a tight budget, you may choose to use green lumber. Be fore-warned, though—cracks will develop between siding boards and in other places, since green lumber shrinks as it dries. If you decide to go with green lumber, be sure to use only galvanized nails, as untreated nails will ease out of the wood as the lumber shrinks. Also, if you are not using the green lumber right away, store it in piles that are "stickered," by placing a small piece of 1" or 2" wood between the boards to avoid cracking and warping while the wood dries.

Lumber which has been kiln-dried and milled to exact dimensions is called (surprise!) kiln-dried lumber. Handsome, durable, readily available almost any-where, and easy to work with, it is most often used to build sheds. Kiln-dried softwood dimensional lumber, as we've suggested using for your shed's trim, roof decking, and much of its framing, comes in a variety of grades—industry standards that indi-cate its type, appearance, and defects. A *common* grade, with the greatest number of defects, is the least expensive; a *clear* grade is nearly defect-free, but will cost quite a bit more. In between a common and clear grade are a variety of other grades, and there is some variation of quality within grades, so when you bring your materials list to a salesperson, it's not a bad idea to pick the lumber with them, so that you get the best boards and timbers available. Excepting the most costly clear grades, any grade of wood will include *knots*, where limbs once grew from the tree's trunk; these won't affect your shed's structural integrity or appearance. When checking lumber for defects, keep an eye out for *checks*, which are cracks at the lumber's end which can develop into splits along the grain; *wane*, when the ends

become rounded from certain sawing methods; and *warpage*, when a piece of lumber is bent or twisted. If you choose not to use the plywood siding we've suggested, and plan to install board-and-batten, shiplapped, or other board siding, avoid buying boards with stains, grade stamps, or insect holes.

For all softwood boards and timbers in contact with soil, a concrete foundation, and especially water, pressure-treated lumber will work best and last longest, keeping out moisture and termites. Pressure-treated wood has been treated with Fluor Chrome Arsenate Phenol (FCAP) or a Chromated Copper Arsenate process (these are water-borne preservatives that contain inorganic arsenic and are safe for home use). For framing and other aboveground purposes, wood that has undergone a light-density treatment is

## SOFTWOOD LUMBER SIZES

| NOMINAL | ACTUAL |
|---------|--------|
| 1 x 2 | ¾" x 1½" |
| 1 x 4 | ¾" x 3½" |
| 1 x 6 | ¾" x 5½" |
| 1 x 8 | ¾" x 7¼" |
| 1 x 10 | ¾" x 9¼" |
| 1 x 12 | ¾" x 11¼" |
| 2 x 2 | 1½" x 1½" |
| 2 x 4 | 1½" x 3½" |
| 2 x 6 | 1½" x 5½" |
| 2 x 8 | 1½" x 7¼" |
| 2 x 10 | 1½" x 9¼" |
| 2 x 12 | 1½" x 11¼" |
| 4 x 4 | 3-½" x 3½" |
| 4 x 6 | 3½" x 5½" |
| 6 x 6 | 5½" x 5½" |
| 8 x 8 | 7½" x 7½" |

more than adequately resistant to decay. We've suggested using pressure-treated pine to frame the base of your shed; if you live in an especially wet or rainy area, or near the ocean, you may want to use pressure-treated wood for all the framing and siding. Pressure-treated lumber can cost up to twice as much as untreated lumber, but is a smart investment. You'll be putting a lot of time into building your shed, and you want it to give you lots of good years of use in return.

## PLYWOOD

To side and floor your shed, we've suggested using plywood, which is lighter and cheaper than most solid woods and very easy to work with. Plywood is made of *plies*, or thin layers of wood, aligned and glued together; as a rule, the core layer is lumber or manufactured wood, and the outer layers are higher-quality and look better. There are two basic types of plywood: construction plywood and hardwood plywood. Construction plywood is made of softwood or hardwood or both, and is sold in 4' x 8' panels, in thicknesses of ¼", ½", and ¾". It is made in exterior and interior types. You'll use CDX construction plywood for the floor of your shed, and T1-11 plywood for siding. The wood grain of plywood, of course, is not quite as beautiful as that of natural softwood or hardwood boards, but when it's finished well with paint or stain, plywood can look equally attractive.

## DIMENSION LUMBER

Building with kiln-dried and pressure-treated softwood boards and plywood means you will be working with dimension lumber. Dimension lumber comes in sizes ranging from 1 x 2 to 8 x 8, usually in lengths ranging from eight to 20'. Excluding siding and flooring, you will be using dimension lumber for all the jobs required to complete your shed. When working with dimension lumber, it is important to understand and remember that the sizes commonly referred to—a 2 x 4, say, or a 1 x 6—are not the actual sizes of the boards you are buying. In the building industry, these dimensions are referred to as *nominal*. In fact, a 2 x 4 is actually 1½" x 3½", and a 1 x 6 is actually ¾" x 5½". While this may seem like

a cruel and unnecessary trick, the reason for the discrepancy between nominal and actual dimensions is logical. Some years back, the building industry's load requirements for

FACE
EDGE
ARRIS
END

lumber were cut to the material's maximum load-bearing capacity. The chart opposite will familiarize you with nominal versus actual dimensions. Look it over, and if you're new to working with dimension lumber, stay alert to the discrepancies as you are building, so that you don't find yourself momentarily panicking because your lumber seems to be too small.

## PARTS OF A BOARD

Different steps in any construction process require that boards and timbers be arranged, laid, and fastened with different parts of them meeting parts of other boards. While the architectural plans and common sense usually make it clear how the board should be positioned relative to its own shape, there are times when it can be confusing to figure out how a board or timber should be placed. It's helpful to know the proper terms commonly used to describe the different parts of dimension lumber: *face, edge, arris*, and *end*. Faces are the wider surfaces on opposite sides of a board (the 4" side of a 2 x 4, for example), or on all sides of square-sectioned lumber such as a 4 x 4. Edges are the other sides, the narrow sides adjacent to the faces (the 2" side of a 2 x 4). The ends, of course, are easy. When following our how-to instructions, you won't be much concerned with *arrises*—the junctures between faces and edges (or between faces on square stock). But again, if this is your first Adventure in Building, it's good to get all the basics straight before you get started.

Typically, permanent foundations for sheds are made of concrete blocks, or poured concrete slabs or piers. Because concrete pier foundations can be set to adapt to varying frost depths (and so can be used in any geography), we've suggested using them for the building projects offered in this book. Pier foundations are vertical building supports resting on individual footings, spaced beneath interior construction, around the structure's perimeter; the dimensions and spacing of the piers depend on the building's structural load and the underlying earth's load-bearing capacity. The piers are formed by pouring concrete into cylindrical forms made of waxed, heavy-duty cardboard.

■

## CONCRETE

To build the sheds in this book, you will be using 8" cardboard forms, and will need to hand-mix and pour a relatively small amount of concrete. For our Potting Shed and Storage Shed, and others using six 8" cardboard forms to create the pier foundation, you'll need 12 40# bags of standard pre-mixed concrete—approximately two bags per cardboard form. Concrete generally comes in lb-bags from 10–to 80#, with the price decreasing as the pound load per bag increases. Bags of concrete are awkward to haul around, and a 60- or 80# bag can throw your back out fast if you're unaccustomed to hefting heavy objects. Purchasing 40# bags will make the task a lot easier and not drive the cost up more than a few dollars.

Mixing concrete is easy, and bags of premixed concrete include detailed manufacturer's instructions on the back. Just pour the premixed substance into a tall-sided wheelbarrow and add water slowly, mixing with a shovel, until the concrete reaches a fluid, but thick consistency. Mix enough concrete to fill only one cardboard form at a time, and do not make your concrete too soupy, or slushy, or it won't harden properly. Once you've got the right mix, you can pour the concrete directly from the wheelbarrow into the cardboard form, or, in the interest of cau-

tion, use a shovel to transfer the concrete from wheelbarrow to cardboard form.

■

## GRAVEL

There isn't much to say about so basic a substance. You'll use it to pack the bottom of your pier holes, to help stabilize the cardboard forms placed therein. A small 10# bag of #80 gravel mix will do the trick.

■

## CYLINDRICAL CARDBOARD FORMS

These forms or tubes come in standard lengths, and diameters ranging from 8" on up. In laying your foundation, you will need to place them in holes of appropriate depths calculated to adapt to frost depth temperatures in your area, and cut them to varying heights to make the foundation level. Your crosscut handsaw will cut them easily, although using a circular saw will make a cleaner cut.

■

## POST ANCHORS

Post anchors are metal fasteners that, fixed in concrete by anchor bolts, hold the timbers which form the base of a structure. They come in different sizes, but the 4" x 4" model, which you'll use when constructing your shed, are common and easy to find.

**S**heds can be built with many different roof styles. All of the shed styles we've offered are variations on simple 8' x 10' sheds with either shed or gable roofs, which are constructionally simple and have broad appeal. Whether you choose one of these roof styles, or opt to build a shed with a gambrel or other type of roof, you'll need to choose roofing material that suits your shed's needs and appearance.

The gentle, intricate off-rhythms of rain dancing on a tin roof soothe and mesmerize, and we've used a "tin" roof to top off our Potting Shed. (In fact, what most of us see and believe to be "tin" roofs, nowadays, are actually made from galvanized and corrugated steel or aluminum.) The plans and specifications for some of the shed variations in this book call for using a range of roofing materials and styles, techniques for all of which we can't address at length in a book of this size. The information below will guide you through purchasing and using some basic roofing materials and the type of metal roofing we've chosen.

**▪**

## FELT ROLL-ROOFING

Between the roof's wood decking and metal roofing, you'll install a layer of felt roofing material to act as a buffer between the decking boards and metal, and to provide additional protection against moisture damage. Felt roll-roofing comes in 3'-wide rolls cut to length. It's easy to cut and is secured with small roofing tacks.

**▪**

## METAL ROOFING

Lots of different metals make durable and attractive roofs: aluminum and steel, terne (lead-and-tin-coated steel), tin, and copper (requiring professional installation), as well as aluminum and steel roofing manufactured to simulate wood shingles and clay tiles. We've used corrugated, or "ribbed," aluminum, which will last for decades if properly installed and is available in lots of colors. We chose "ocean blue," but both steel and aluminum roofing come in a spectrum of colors that coordinate with lots of color schemes. (Roofing made of these metals can also be purchased "raw" and then painted.) Aluminum and steel roofing come in standard sizes which must usually be ordered through a building supplier; with luck, your local supplier will be able to provide you with a sheet of roofing precut to your roof's exact

**▪**

## RAFTER TIES

Easy to use, these lightweight fasteners help place and secure rafters. They come in standard sizes and are affixed to the wood rafters by nailing through small holes predrilled by the manufacturer.

the door's thickness, width, and composition. Secondly most hinges are specified as either right-handed or left-handed, and determine the door's swing accordingly. If your door will open out to the right, as the door of our Potting Shed does, make sure you buy *left-hand* hinges; *right-hand* hinges should be used for doors opening out to the left. There are also a number of different types of door latches, bolts, and handles, from high-security, burglar-proof models to utterly basic sliding bolts. We've used inexpensive steel hinges, door handles, and other pieces of hardware to fasten the door and fold-out potting shelf/window on our Potting Shed.

Before selecting your hardware, shop around in stores and hardware catalogues to get a sense of what type of hardware will best complement the appearance of your finished shed. Do you want a no-frills latch or hook? A more historic-looking strap hinge or wrought-iron latch? An ordinary mortise or cylindrical lock set, as you would find on a house door? A plain old padlock? Make a thumbnail sketch of the door and window with the hardware, and show it to a salesperson. He or she will be able to help you

dimensions. Otherwise, you will have to cut the roofing with a circular saw and special, metal-cutting blade before you install it.

## MATERIALS FOR DOORS AND WINDOWS

**W**hichever shed you choose to build, you will need to choose various pieces of hardware to attach and facilitate the opening and closing of windows and doors. All hardware components come in an extensive range of materials and styles, from low-cost steel from the corner hardware store's bargain bin, to reproduction historic forged iron. If you know exactly what you want, antique stores and architectural salvage companies can also produce pieces that will give a special touch to your finished shed's overall look. Likewise, just about any kind of glass can be used for windows, as long as it's installed properly.

■

### HINGES AND HANDLES

Hinges are available in many shapes, sizes, metals, and finishes, and that part of the choosing is entirely up to you. There are a couple of things to bear in mind when buying a hinge. First, the hinges must be able to support the door's weight, letting it still swing easily. Make sure you select hinges that accommodate

choose the hinges and handles that serve your shed's aesthetic and functional requirements.

■

### CHAIN

One of the nicest features of our Potting Shed is its indoor/outdoor potting shelf, which folds neatly back into the shed's front wall. If you opt to build this shed, you'll need a length of metal chain, about six feet long, to fasten the shelf to the wall structure, so that it can fold in and out. Any strong, attractive type of chain will work. Since the chain will show when the shelf is folded down for use, choose one that looks good with your other hardware.

■

### GLASS AND PLEXIGLASS

The type of glass you use in the windows and door(s) of your shed depends on what look you prefer. Antique panes of stained, colored, or even clear glass can add an elegant touch to a back yard structure, but may be difficult for new builders to cut and handle. If you opt to use new, clear glass, either standard plate glass or Plexiglass is fine (you may want to get plate glass cut to fit). We've used Plexiglass, which is slightly more expensive than plate glass, but wonderfully resists breakage and midflight neighborhood baseballs!

# FASTENERS AND MISCELLANEOUS MATERIALS

■

### WOOD GLUE

Carpenter's wood glue is often used as a temporary or additional fastener for some framing and roofing jobs. When installing felt roll-roofing to the wood roof sheathing, applying beads of glue to the boards will help secure the felt before you nail it. Likewise, when you are attaching the plywood floor to the floor joists, beading the joists with glue will help hold the plywood in place as you nail it down. In both instances, a heavy-duty construction or wood glue will work best. This glue comes in both squeeze bottles and canisters that fit into a glue gun that works like a caulking gun (this is not a hot-glue gun). Either will work fine for these purposes, though a glue gun will speed the process.

### NAILS

Because the building techniques we've used are aimed at maximum simplicity, the bulk of your fastening needs will be met by using simple common nails. Common nails are used for general purposes in all types of heavy construction, and have large heads which won't pull through the fastened wood. Common and most other nails come in a range of

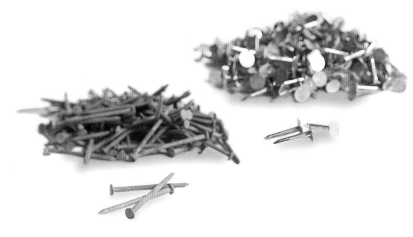

lengths from 1" to 6", with their diameters increasing slightly with length. The length of a common nail is described by its "penny size": A 1" common nail, for example, is also called a "twopenny nail" or a "2d nail." For these projects, you will use mostly 16d nails and lighter weight 8d and 6d siding nails, along with small 1¼" roofing tacks. It's wise to use galvanized nails, which are coated with zinc and will hold up better against rust and corrosion, throughout the shed's construction. If you choose to use ordinary nails for some of the work, be sure to use galvanized nails for exterior siding and trim.

## WOOD SCREWS

Otherwise called "flathead" screws, wood screws are general-purpose screws driven flush with a surface or countersunk just below the surface. Like most types of screws, wood screws come in lengths up to 6" and in a range of diameters.

## DRYWALL SCREWS

Drywall screws have a bugle-shaped head and are thin, sharp, and hardened, with deep threads to cut into boards and studs. You'll use these only for your temporary structure of batter boards.

## LAG BOLTS

Lag bolts, also called lag screws, are heavy-duty wood screws that come in lengths up to 6". Attached with a wrench or ratchet and socket, they are ideal for hanging heavy objects such as doors.

## JOIST HANGERS AND JOIST HANGER NAILS

These small metal brackets fit snugly around the underside of a floor joist or other horizontal stud to give extra support and to help fasten the joist to other framing members. Special joist hanger nails are driven through predrilled holes in the hanger to secure it to the joist or stud.

## VINYL Z-FLASHING

Cheap, flexible, and easy to install, this material comes in a standard size and is fashioned to fit closely around the edge of plywood or thin boards and protect against moisture damage where two sheets of plywood or other boards meet on an exterior wall.

## FINISHES

As this book's section on decorating ready-made or kit sheds makes clear, there are many more ways than one to finish a shed! Given the vast range of colors for paints and stains (and even roofs) available, finishing and trim techniques, types of hardware and other details, almost any structure can be made to look any way. If you aren't very familiar with finishing materials, it helps to have a well-formed idea of the overall effect you want for your shed's appearance. Again, making a sketch is a good idea (even if it's a bad sketch!). Then, with just a little research, you can determine which exact materials will help you achieve the look you want.

## PAINTS AND STAINS

Exterior paints and stains will both protect your shed's exterior surfaces from the

elements, and enhance the structure's overall appearance. Even if the final look you're after is rustic and weathered, it's a smart move to finish your shed, since any exposed wood will begin to lose its hue in a year or so. Exterior finishes can be divided into two main types—water-based, or latex, and oil- or solvent-based, also called alkyd. Latex paints and stains are generally easier to apply, and you can clean and thin them with water (siding manufacturers sometimes warn against using oil-based paints); a medium- to high-quality latex finish will last for several years. Stains, whether latex or alkyd, come in solid, semi-transparent, and transparent types: a solid stain will cover a surface almost like a paint, giving a nearly opaque color. Transparent stains contain very little pigment, and show off a wood's grain and textures—they are better used with woods that are naturally highly attractive.

Often, paint is suggested as the best finish for plywood siding such as we've suggested using, since plywood's raw appearance is less than optimal. We've used a semitransparent stain, though, which colors the wood while still showing some of the grain, and the result is surprisingly attractive. If you haven't done much exterior finish work, consult a clerk at the paint store or home improvement center; have them help you choose the paintbrushes and roller that will work best. If you're using a latex finish, you can use a brush with synthetic or natural bristles; if you decide to go with an alkyd finish, a brush with natural bristles will work better. Last, don't skimp on buying a brush. Cheap paintbrushes leave bristles in the finish, which not only mars the finished surface, but can be highly frustrating—you want to paint, not pick, after all.

■

## TRIM

Even if you're an inexperienced carpenter and are sticking to bare-bones techniques, you can easily add stylistic flourishes to your shed by adding unusual or stylized trim. We've trimmed our potting shed with a straightforward casing-style trim. There are a number of other styles of trim, many of which the techniques are not too tricky to master with a good all-around finishing manual and some persistence. For those who don't do well with more intricate woodworking, many home improvement centers carry lengths of prefashioned trim which can be purchased very reasonably.

# THE SHED-ROOFED
# POTTING SHED

### AND FOUR VARIATIONS

Now that you are generally acquainted with the tools, materials, and skills you need to build your shed, you're ready to actually start construction. In this chapter you'll find explicitly detailed instructions on how to build our Potting Shed, a simple 8' x 10' structure capped with a classic shed roof. The instructions, written to take absolute beginners with virtually no foreknowledge of wood-working or carpentry techniques or terms through the construction process from start to finish, are accompanied by how-to photos and a complete materials list. Architectural plans for the Potting Shed are on pages 111-114 of the plans section (see figs 1-16).

There's more to come than pure pragmatism and a single shed, though. "Variety is the soul of pleasure," wrote the brilliant and notorious 17th-century English poetess Aphra Behn, and along those lines, we've provided four variations on the Potting Shed's basic roofline and structure. While dyed-in-the-wool backyard builders will find construction for all of the variations straightforward and easy, some variations might not be the best choice for first-timers to build, as their constructions do require some additional skills and carpentry savoir faire. But whether your tastes run to traditional, contemporary, or romantic, you'll be sure to find inspiration and ideas in these four good-looking, multifunctional structures.

## POTTING SHED

This handsome, unpretentious little potting shed is perfect for gardeners with small-item storage needs, who like to putter both inside and outside with their seeds, soil, and terra cotta pots. Its unique fold-out worktable allows you to work outdoors on those balmy spring and ethereal autumn days, yet work under shelter when the wind kicks up or a light afternoon shower tests your patience just a bit. Better yet, once you've come in out of the weather, you'll

be treated to the enchanting lilt of raindrops on the metal roof.

Of course, before you get your fingers into the potting soil, you'll have to slip them around your hammer handle. But as long as you've gathered all of your materials and tools—or those you'll need for the first stage of construction—you're ready to go. Whistle the first note of your favorite work tune, and let the building begin!

# MATERIALS AND SUPPLIES

## LUMBER

| DESCRIPTION | QTY. | MATERIAL | DIMENSIONS |
|---|---|---|---|
| Batter boards | 5 | 1 x 4s (any type) | 12' long |
| Base | 1 | pressure-treated pine 4 x 6 | 16' long |
| | 2 | pressure-treated pine 4 x 6s | 10' long |
| Floor | 7 | pressure-treated pine 2 x 6s | 8' long |
| | 1 | pressure-treated pine 2 x 6 | 10' long |
| | 3 | CDX plywood | 4' x 8' |
| Wall framing | 16 | spruce 2 x 4s | 10' long |
| | 13 | spruce 2 x 4s | 12' long |
| | 30 | spruce 2 x 6s | 8' long |
| | 3 | spruce 2 x 6s | 10' long |
| | 2 | spruce 2 x 4s | 6' long |
| Roof rafters | 6 | spruce 2 x 6s | 12' long |
| Rafter blocking | 1 | spruce 2 x 4 | 10' long |
| Roof decking | 14 | tongue-and-groove spruce 2 x 6s | 12' long |
| Wall siding | 9 | T1-11 plywood | 4' x 8' |
| Trim | 4 | cedar 1 x 4s | 10' long |
| | 6 | cedar 1 x 4s | 8' long |
| | 4 | cedar 1 x 8s | 12' long |
| | 1 | cedar 2 x 4 | 8' long |
| Lookouts | 2 | spruce 2 x 4s | 12' long |
| Door | 1 | spruce 2 x 4 | 14' long |
| | 1 | spruce 2 x 4 | 12' long |
| | 1 | cedar 1 x 4 | 10' long |
| Window | 1 | cedar 2 x 4 | 8' long |
| | | | |
| Batter boards | 1 | mason's line | |
| Foundation | 6 | cylindrical cardboard forms | 8" diameter |
| | 12 | bags premixed concrete | 40# |
| | 1 | bag gravel | 40# |
| Roofing | 80' | felt roll-roofing | 3' wide |
| | 1 | presized metal roof | 12' x 11' 10½" |
| Siding | 15' | standard z-flashing | |
| Vents | 10 | rectangular metal vents | 4" x 16" |
| Windows | 1 | Plexiglass sheet | 4' x 4' |

## FASTENERS

- 1 box 1½" drywall screws
- 10 boxes 2" galvanized 16d nails
- 14 standard-size joist hangers
- 1 box joist hanger nails
- 10 4" x 4" adjustable post anchors
- 1 box ½" anchor bolts
- 1 box 1¼" roofing tacks
- 2 boxes galvanized 8d siding nails
- 1 box galvanized 6d siding nails
- 1 box ½" wood screws
- 1 box 1⅝" wood screws
- 5 hinges
- 5 1½" ⁵⁄₁₆ diameter lag bolts
- 1 length metal chain
- 1 bottle construction wood glue

■

## LAYING OUT YOUR SHED

The first step in the construction of your shed is transferring the layout on paper of six concrete piers to actual points on the ground. This is done by using *batter boards* and mason's line (string), which will be set up to indicate the center of each concrete pier.

Batter boards consist of two 1 x 4s, called ledgers, set at a right angle and nailed to three 1 x 4 stakes. This formation allows a mason's line to be adjusted in order to precisely locate the six center points for the concrete piers. Since the batter boards will be used only temporarily, they need not be constructed from pressure-treated wood—any type of lumber will work.

To ensure that your foundation lays out as shown in fig. 1, it is important to follow these steps closely.

**1.** Determine which direction your shed will face, considering window and door locations, and the roofline. Referring to figs. 13-16 use four stones or other objects identified as A, B, C, and D to roughly

locate the corners of your shed's position. Corners A and C will mark the 8' side of your shed where the door and fold-out potting shelf/window are located.

**2.** Cut 20 1 x 4s approximately 2'–3' long, and sharpen 12 at one end. Leave the remaining eight with their ends square. You'll need three sharpened boards for stakes, and two uncut boards for ledgers at each corner, to set up your batter boards.

**3.** At corner A, drive three stakes into the ground approximately 18" apart, to form a right angle 1'-2' outside of corner A. Drive the stakes 8"–12" into the ground until they are reasonably stable. Using a drill and one 1½" drywall screw, attach one end of a ledger to the top of an outside stake. Raise this ledger until it is level, and attach with two drywall

**4.** Drive three stakes into the ground outside of the remaining corners B, C, and D, in the same right-angle configuration as at corner A. Do not attach ledgers at these corners yet.

**5.** Tie one end of a length of string to the ledger at corner A that faces corner B. Keeping the string taut, stretch the string to the corner stake at corner B. Place a line level on this string line A-B. When the line level indicates that string line A-B stretched to the corner stake at corner B is level, mark the corner stake at this height with a pencil. Using the same method you used at corner A, attach two ledgers to the stakes at corner B at this height. Using your line level and 4' level, make sure that the ledgers at corners A and B are level with each other. Tie the string you have stretched from corner A to the ledger at corner B and leave in place. (See photos 3 and 4.)

**6.** Repeat step 4 and step 5 to corners C and D. When you are finished, all eight batter boards should be level with each other. The four strings you have attached across the corners will be in place.

**7.** The next step is to begin to check that all four string lines, A-B, B-D, D-C, and C-A, are at right angles to each other, by using what is known as the *contractors' 3-4-5 measuring technique*. At corner A, mark the strings at the point where they cross to indicate the proposed center of the concrete pier. Starting at this marked intersection, measure 3' out on one string, and 4' out on the other. The diagonal distance between these two points should be exactly 5'. If this distance is greater or smaller than 5', adjust the strings right or left on the batter boards as needed to achieve a 5' measurement. The point where the two strings cross at a right angle is the center of the concrete pier that will be located at corner A. We'll call it point A; now that point A is established, tie off and secure lines A-B and C-A. We will measure from point A to locate points B, C, and D at the other corners.

**8.** From point A, measure 9' 4" along string A-B toward corner B and mark this point on the string (see photo 5). This mark indicates Point B on the

screws to the corner stake; now secure the first end of the ledger with a second drywall screw (see photo 2). Nailing into the end of the board, attach the second ledger to the corner stake and the other outside stake at the same height and level as the first ledger. These ledgers must be level, as the ledgers at the remaining three corners will be attached at the same height. Corner A is now the reference height for the remaining three corners B, C, and D.

first string. Slide string B-D along its batter boards until it coincides with point B as marked on string A-B. Tie off and secure string line B-D at the corner B batter boards. Moving string line B-D from the far end of the string (the batter boards at corner D), use the 3-4-5 method to establish a right angle at point B. Tie off and secure line B-D at corner D's batter boards.

**9.** Measure from point B 7' 8" along string line B-D and mark this point on the string. This is point D. Using the 3-4-5 method, adjust line D-C to establish and fix point D at a right angle. Tie off and secure line D-C at corner D. Measure 9' 4" from point D along string D-C. This is point C, which should cross line C-A precisely 7' 4" from point A, at a right angle. Confirm the right angle using the 3-4-5 method. If you do not have a right angle at this point, loosen string C-A at corner C and pinch both strings between your thumb and forefinger at point C. Slide the strings on both ledgers simultaneously until a right angle is achieved. Tie off and secure the strings at corner C.

**10.** To confirm that points A, B, C, and D as you have located them create a perfect rectangle, measure diagonally from point A to point D, and then from point B to C. The diagonal distances between each pair of points should be equivalent (an inch difference is okay). (See photos 6 and 7.)

**11.** Now that you have located the four corner points, you can easily locate the two mid-points, shown as C1 and A1 (see fig. 1). Measure 4' 8" (this is halfway) from point A along line A-B, and mark this point on the string. Repeat this process on line B-D. These six points indicate the exact centers for the concrete piers.

**12.** Next, using a plumb bob, transfer these six points as marked on the strings to points on the ground. Each of these points represents the center of a pier around which you will be digging a hole, so you may want to first clear any vegetation, exposing the dirt that will surround each point. To transfer the

8

10

11

points, hold the plumb bob's string against the marks on the line and let the point of the suspended plumb bob fall to the ground (see photo 8). Using a stick, nail, or your finger, draw a rough 10"–12" circle around the point where the plumb bob rests. Repeat this process at all six points. Mark the tops of all eight ledgers at the point where the string is secured to it. Then loosen each line at one end of each of the four string lines (either end is fine) to make it easier to excavate the holes.

**13.** Using a shovel, posthole digger, or power auger, dig a hole 10"–12" in diameter using your circumscribed rough circle as a guide (see photos 9 and 10). This hole must be deeper than the frost line in your area (see photo 11). Tighten the strings back into position after digging your holes.

9

■

## PREPPING THE CONCRETE PIERS

The foundation for your shed will consist of six 8"-diameter concrete piers set into the ground. To create these concrete piers, a hollow, 8"-diameter cardboard form, or tube, will be placed in each of the holes you have dug. These will be filled with concrete to a uniform level, stabilized by backfilling around the tube, and fitted with anchor bolts and post anchors in which you will lay boards, to begin to frame the base of your shed.

**14.** Before placing the tubes in the holes, determine whether you will need to place a layer of tightly packed gravel beneath them. Four inches of packed gravel is recommended for soft or sandy soils; if necessary, place a layer of gravel in the bottom of each hole. Starting with hole A, place a tube in the hole, then measure and mark a line on the tube 1" above the ground at the point where the soil is highest on the side of the tube. Remove the tube from the hole and, using a tape measure, measure the distance between the top end of the tube and the mark you have made. Measure and mark this same distance from the top end of the tube around the circumference of the tube. These marks will serve as your guide for cutting the tube to a level height. Using your crosscut handsaw, carefully cut the tube.

**15.** Place the tube in the hole with the cut end down, manufactured end up. Using the marks you have made on your ledger boards as a guide, reattach all of your string lines. Center the tube in hole A on point A as marked on the string lines. Using a 4' level, make sure that the top of the tube is level. Measure the distance from the strings to the bottom of the 4' level (see photo 12). This measurement denotes the distances from the level string lines to the tops of all six tubes, which must all be the same (or your building will slope in unimaginable directions!). Measure the same distance from the line level to points on the uncut tubes. Mark these points. Using the same technique you used in step 14, cut these five tubes.

**16.** Now, place each tube with the manufactured end up in a hole. Center each tube according to the center points on the string lines. Using a 4' level, ensure that the tops of all the tubes are level and equidistant from the string.

**17.** As in step 12, loosen each line at one end of each of the four string lines (either end is fine). Backfill between the tube and the earth with firmly packed dirt, or #2 crushed stone. This will keep the forms from moving around as they are filled with concrete.

**18.** You can now disassemble the four batter boards and the string lines, which you will no longer need.

### POURING THE CONCRETE PIERS

Now that the cardboard forms are in place, you're ready to pour the concrete. Note: You'll need to let the concrete set for 48 hours before continuing work, so relax and rest for a day or two!

**19.** Following the mixing instructions on the bag of premixed concrete, mix only the amount of concrete needed for one hole at a time. First, mix with water the contents of two 40# bags of premixed concrete in a level, stable wheelbarrow. Starting with any tube, carefully fill it with mixed concrete, leaving some excess at the top (see photo 13).

**20.** Using a 2 x 4, screed the excess concrete across the top of the filled tube until the surface is level.

**21.** Depending on which tube you have chosen to fill with concrete and fit with an anchor bolt first, you may need one or two anchor bolts for the pier.

**14**

**15**

**16**

Each corner pier will need two anchor bolts; the intermediate piers will require only one. (See fig.2 for all corner piers A, B, C, D and fig. 3, for intermediate piers A1 and C1.) Place a ½" x 6" anchor bolt in the wet concrete with the threads up approximately ¾"-1" above the concrete surface (see fig.4). The dimension of the anchor bolt exposed above the concrete pier can vary from manufacturer to manufacturer. Measure in from the sides of the tube to ensure the anchor bolt is placed correctly as shown in figs. 2 and 3.

**22.** Repeat this process, adapting it according to the above-described distinctions between corner and intermediate piers, for the remaining five piers.

**23.** Allow 48 hours for the concrete to set before proceeding.

■

## FRAMING THE BASE

■ Beginning with this section and throughout the remaining instructions, the four walls of shed will be referred to as A-C, B-A, D-B, and C-D.

*Note: For steps 24–57, you will be using galvanized 16d nails as fasteners, unless others are specified.*

**24.** Referring to figs. 2,3, and 4 on page 111, place a 4" x 4" post anchor on each of the ½" anchor bolts per manufacturer's instructions. These are made to allow adjustment, so only hand tighten. (See photos 14, 15, and 16.)

**25.** Next, cut one 16'-long 4 x 6 exactly in half. Starting at the front side A-C, place one of these 8'-long 4 x 6s face down in each post anchor. Hammer a few nails through the side of the post anchor into the 4 x 6 to temporarily hold it in position. Repeat this process for side D-B.

**26.** Select two 10'-long 4 x 6s. Cut 8" off the end of one of these 4 x 6s, and place this 9' 4"-long 4 x 6 face down in the post anchors along side C-D, across intermediate pier C1. Hammer a few nails through the side of each post anchor into the 4 x 6 to temporarily hold it in position. Repeat this process for the opposite side B-A, across intermediate post A1.

**27.** Now check to ensure that the base is square by using the 3-4-5 technique. If necessary, make lateral adjustments to the temporarily secured base by sliding the post anchors. (These anchors have oversized holes at their bases which allow them to be moved slightly relevant to the fixed anchor bolts.) Also, check the two diagonal dimensions of your base; each should measure 12' 9$\frac{11}{16}$".

**28.** When the base is square, tighten all the anchor

bolts and hammer nails through the remaining holes in the post anchors into the 4 x 6s that now form your base (see photo 17).

■

### FRAMING AND DECKING THE FLOOR

*Note:* **The sub-floor also serves as the interior floor for this shed, the Storage Shed, and all variations. If you prefer a more finished look for the interior floor, you can frame the floor as described below, then use pressure-treated wood boards to deck the floor. You will need twenty 10'-long ⁵⁄₄" x 6" pressure-treated wood decking boards.**

**29.** Starting with side B-A, measure from the outside corner of the base at corner A to the outside corner of the base at corner B; this measurement will be exactly 10 ', or 120". (See photo 18.) Using a carpenter's pencil, mark the inside face of the 4 x 6 every 16" up to and including the 96" point. Make another mark at the 108" point. These seven marks identify the center points for placement of the floor joists. Measure ¾" out on each side from each of these seven marks; using your speed or framing square to make precise vertical marks, make two new marks on either side of the original seven marks (see photo 19). These new marks, which will be 1½" apart from one another, serve as alignment guides for placement of the floor joists.

**30.** Repeat this process on side C-D, beginning measurement from corner C.

**31.** Cut seven 8'-long 2 x 6s to 89"; these are the floor joists. First, use the toenailing method to secure each joist to sides B-A and C-D of the base at the guideline marks you have made (see photo 20), then attach each with two joist hangers (one on each end). Use at least eight joist-hanger nails to hold each joist hanger in place (see photo 21).

**32.** The next step is blocking the floor joists, to stabilize the center of the floor. First, cut six 14½"-long 2 x 6s; one 10½"-long 2 x 6; and one 7¾"-long

2 x 6. Using two nails on each end of each block, nail this blocking between the joists, along the approximate center perpendicular to the joists (see photo 22).

**33.** To prepare the floor framing for the plywood floor, apply a generous bead of wood glue to the tops of the base and joists (see photo 23). Lay one uncut sheet of plywood flush and square with corner A, and lengthwise along side B-A (see photo 24). Spacing nails approximately 12" apart, nail the plywood to the joists. Make sure the middle joist 96" from the end of the base is bisected evenly by the end of this piece of plywood. Lay a second uncut sheet of plywood next to the first, flush and square with corner C, lengthwise along side C-D. Like the first, this sheet of plywood should evenly bisect the 96" joist. Last, cut one sheet of plywood to 2' x 8'. If all of your measurements so far are correct, this piece laid perpendicular will meet the ends of the other two pieces of plywood across the 96" joist, and fit. (To be on the safe side, measure the remaining uncovered joists first, then cut the plywood to fit.) (See photo 25.)

■

### FRAMING WALL C-D

(See fig.8)

Now that your foundation and floor are in place, you're ready to frame the walls of your shed. Using the structure you have just built as a building platform, build the walls horizontally, then raise them to their vertical position.

**34.** First, select two 10'-long 2 x 4s. One of these will be the bottom plate for this wall; the other will be the sill for the window openings. Lay these 2 x 4s next to one another face up on a flat surface (see photo 26). Referring to fig. 8, measure and mark the locations for nine wall studs—these marks must be made 16" on center. For correct placement of the marks, lay your tape across one of the boards from one end to the other. With your carpenter's pencil, mark the following inch points along the board: 3", 12", 28", 44", 60", 76", 92 ", 108", and 115½". Using your framing square as a guide, draw a line across the faces of both boards at each of the points marked. Make a second mark exactly 1½" to the right of each of these marks, and draw an X between each set of marks on both boards (see photo 27). The Xs mark the locations of the wall studs.

**35.** Take one of these marked 10'-long 2 x 4s and, using a handsaw or circular saw, cut 3" off each end; this 9' 6"-long 2 x 4 will be your sill plate. Next, select five 12'-long 2 x 4s; from these, cut nine pieces 5' 4" long. (You'll have four pieces approximately 16" long, and one piece approximately 6' 8" left over; save these to use for later steps in framing this wall.) Lay the uncut, marked 10'-long 2 x 4 (bottom plate) on edge approximately along side C-D of your base platform, and lay the cut 9' 6"-long 2 x 4 (sill for windows) on edge approximately 5' 6" away from the bottom plate, toward side B-A. The X marks should be facing each other; lay the nine studs on edge in the proper locations.

**36.** Next, cut four 8'-long 2 x 4s, and lay two on edge at each side to frame the outside of the sill plate, bottom plate, and wall studs. Using a framing square, align the base plate and outside double studs. To secure this structure, begin by nailing the outside studs to one another, and to the bottom plate and sill plate, to form a square frame. Nail this structure so that it is square and secure. Confirm the alignment of the intermediate studs at their marks, and using two nails at each end, nail these studs to the sill and bottom plate (see photo 28). You have now framed the bottom half of the wall.

25

26

27

**37.** The next step is to frame the windows and upper section of the wall. So that the framing section you are working on is on the level platform, move the section you have just completed past the end of wall C-D about 6". Take two 10'-long 2 x 4s and, making sure their placement is square, nail them to

28

29

pieces to fit.) Also, cut twelve 15"-long 2 x 4s; two of these are the "jack studs" (support studs) that will support the header, and the remaining ten are studs that will be used to frame the actual windows. Take two of the 15"-long 2 x 4s and position them on top of the sill plate against the outside double studs at either side of the wall frame; these are the jack studs. Nail the jack studs in place; then lay the header face down on top of them, and toenail it into place. The next step is to position and nail in place the nine 9⅞"-long 2 x 4s, or wall studs, between the header and the doubled top plate. Lay these out at the same dimensions as described in step 34, so that they are 16" on center and exactly aligned with the studs between the sill plate and the bottom plate. Nail the studs in place.

**39.** Next, you will frame the actual windows in the space between the two jack studs supporting the header. This space should be 111" long. Lay your tape along the edge of the sill, and make pencil marks at the following inch points: 6", 21", 27", 42", 48", 63", 69", 84", 90", and 105" (see photo 30). Using a framing square, transfer these marks to lines on the sill's upper face. Then, make another mark 1-½" to the left of each of these lines, and put an X in the space between them. These ten Xs indicate the placement points for the studs that frame the windows. Mark ten points at the same locations on the bottom of the header. Then place the ten 15"-long studs between these sets of marks, and nail them in place (see photo 30 and 31).

**40.** To help raise the wall and stabilize it temporarily while you build and raise the other three walls, you will need to attach a temporary diagonal brace to the outside of this wall. Take a 12'-long 2 x 4 and place it diagonally, approximately from one top corner to another bottom corner of the wall. The placement of this brace does not need to be exact, as long as it is connected to the bottom plate and one set of outside double studs (see photo 32). Next, select two 8'-long 2 x 4s to serve as additional temporary braces. Predrive a single nail into both ends of both braces so that the nails are almost all the way through the 2 x 4s. Nail one end of an 8'-long 2 x 4

the top of the wall frame; this is your double top plate. Select two 10'-long 2 x 6s and cut both to 114". Take a sheet of plywood and cut two 48"-long pieces 5½" wide; from the remainder, cut one 18"-long piece 5½" wide. Placing the three pieces of plywood end to end, sandwich them between the two 2 x 6s and nail them all together (see photo #29). This is your header, which frames the top of the window openings.

**38.** Now, cut nine 9⅞"-long 2 x 4s; these are the walls studs that will be nailed to the header and the doubled top plate, framing the area above the windows. (This 9⅞" dimension is ⅛" less than the dimensions shown on the plans, to allow all of the

to the outside of the platform on side A–C, about 4' from the corner; repeat on side D–B. This single point of attachment will allow the braces to pivot; lay the unattached ends of the braces on the ground. Now, raise wall C–D from the platform to an upright position at the outside edge of the floor. Checking with your 4' level to ensure that the wall frame is plumb, raise the two temporary braces and nail them to the sides of the wall frame (see photo 33). Last, nail the bottom plate of the wall to the floor.

■

### FRAMING AND RAISING WALL B-A

**(See fig.7)**

*Note:* **The process of framing and raising this wall and wall D-B will be much the same as that used to frame wall C-D. Refer to the steps in Framing and Raising Wall C-D while you are framing these two walls.**

**41.** Select three 10'-long 2 x 4s; these will be the bottom plate and doubled top plate for wall B-A. Lay the bottom plate on edge along side B-A, and one of the top plates on edge, parallel and about 6' away from the bottom plate. Cut eleven 5' 6"-long 2 x 4s; these will be the studs for this wall. Cut six 2 x 4s approximately a foot long; these will act as spacers, sandwiched between the two outside studs at each side of the wall frame between the bottom and doubled top plates. With a framing square, align a vertical stud between the outside corner of the top and bottom plates on both sides of the frame.

**34**

Making sure all the corners are square, nail the vertical studs to the top and bottom plates. Next, lay three spacers on edge on one of the vertical studs you have just secured—one at the top, one in the middle, one at the bottom (these locations need not be exact)—and nail these spacers to the stud. Now, take another stud and nail it to the spacers, and to the top and bottom plates. Repeat at the other side of the wall frame. These are the outside stud corners for this wall. Using the same dimensions as you used for placing the studs for wall C-D, mark for the remaining seven studs, and nail them to both plates. The last step is to double the top plate. Lay the remaining 10'-long 2 x 4 on the existing top plate, and nail securely in place.

**42.** Using the same temporary bracing techniques you used to raise and stabilize wall C-D, raise and brace this wall. Remember to use your 4' level to make sure this wall is plumb with the floor before you secure the two pivoting braces. (See photo 34.)

■

### FRAMING AND RAISING WALL D-B

**(See fig. 6)**

*Note:* **While building this wall on the floor, you will use the secured bottom plates of raised walls B-A and C-D as guides to frame the wall.**

**43.** First, cut one 7' 5"-long 2 x 4; this is your bottom plate for wall D-B. Lay this 2 x 4 on edge along side D-B. Starting at corner B, lay your tape along the bottom plate and make marks at 16", 32", 48", 64", and 80". Make another mark $1\frac{1}{2}$" to the left of each of these marks, and draw an X between each set of marks; also, make a mark on the bottom plate $1\frac{1}{2}$" in from each end. These marks indicate locations for this wall's seven wall studs—one outside stud on each side, and five intermediate wall studs. Mark two 8'-long 2 x 4s at 5' $8\frac{1}{2}$", and lay one on edge flush with the inside of the bottom plate for wall B-A. (Set the other marked 2 x 4 aside for now.) Next, mark a 10'-long 2 x 4 at 8' 1½", and lay it on edge and flush with the inside of the bottom plate for wall C-D. Lay the remaining five 8'-long 2 x 4s on edge at their marked stud locations, approximately perpendicular to the bottom plate for wall D-B. Use a chalk line to snap a line between the marks you have made on the two outside studs, at an angle across all seven studs. This line represents the 18½° angle of the 4:12 pitch of the roof. To transfer the angled cut line now marked on the studs' edges to their faces, position your speed square at the low point of the chalk line on each stud, and using the square as a guide, draw a straight line across the face of each stud. Next, set the blade of your circular saw to an 18½° angle, and cut all seven studs on edge from the same direction along the lines you have just drawn on the stud faces. (Remember, an angled cut made to a board's edge is referred to as a beveled cut.) Return the studs to their former positions on edge, aligned with the stud locations you have previously marked.

**44.** Measure the distance between the outsides of your two outside studs; this should be 7' 10", which will be the length of the top plate for this wall. Next, select two 8'-long 2 x 4s and, using your circular saw still set to an 18½° blade angle, cut the 2 x 4s on edge to the length you've just measured, which should be 7' 10", give or take ½". Both ends of each 2 x 4 will be cut at this 18½° bevel. One of these will be the top plate for this wall. (Set the other one aside, to use as the top plate for the remaining wall A-C.) Lay the top plate on edge across the tops of the studs.

**45.** Use your speed square to ensure that each stud as positioned is plumb with the bottom plate. Once they are all plumb, mark the location for each stud on the edge of the top plate. Nail each stud to the top and bottom plates at the marks indicated.

**46.** Raise this wall to its upright position between walls B-A and C-D. Using your 4' level, reconfirm that walls B-A, D-B, and C-D are all plumb, and nail wall D-B to walls B-A and C-D and to the floor flush with its edge. (See photo 35.)5

■
### FRAMING WALL A-C

**(See fig. 6)**

*Note:* **This wall will be built into the existing structure, rather than built on the platform or ground and then raised to upright position.**

**47.** Start by selecting an 8'-long 2 x 4; cut it to 4' 6½". This is the bottom plate for this wall. (There will be no bottom plate where the door is located.) Place it flush with the floor and the outside studs at corner A, and nail it to the studs and floor. Now, take the 8'-long 2 x 4 marked at 5' 8½" that you set aside in step 43, and use your circular saw to cut it at an 18½° bevel. This will be the outside wall stud at the low end of this wall, and will be identical to the corresponding wall stud in wall D-B. Using your 4' level to ensure the stud's placement is plumb, nail this stud on top of the bottom plate to the outside double stud of wall B-A at corner A.

35

**36**

**48.** Select a leftover 2 x 4 at least 20" long (you'll have a few of varying lengths around). Measure from the square end of the 2 x 4 to 18", and mark this point on the 2 x 4. Use your circular saw to cut this end at an 18½° bevel (the 18" mark will be the high end of the bevel's slope). Measure 1½" down on the outside studs of wall C-D, and mark this location. Position the 2 x 4 you've just cut with the long face at this mark, and nail in place.

**49.** Next, select the duplicate 7' 10" 2 x 4 you cut at an 18½° bevel in step 44 and nail across the top of the two outside studs you have framed into wall A-C. This is the top plate for this wall. Measure 1½" from the door opening along the top face of the bottom plate, and mark this point. (Make another mark 1½" to the left of this mark, and draw an X inside, for later stud placement.) Measure up from this point to the bottom of the top plate; the distance should be approximately 7' 1". Select an 8'-long 2 x 4 and measure from the square end to 7' 1". Mark this point, and using this point as the high end

of the stud, cut the 2 x 4 at an 18½° bevel. Place in the stud location you have marked, and use your 4' level to ensure that the placement is plumb. Nail this stud to the top and bottom plates (see photo 36). Confirm the distance from the double stud at corner C to the stud you have just secured. This is your door opening; the distance between these two studs should be 3' 1½".

**50.** Set your circular saw's blade to its normal perpendicular cutting position. Select an 8'-long 2 x 4 and cut two pieces 3' 1½" long. Nail these 2 x 4s together with the ends flush. These will make a header, or horizontal support above the door. Placing the header under and flush with the 18" stud at corner C, use your 4' level to ensure that its placement is level, and nail in place (see photos 37 and 38). Take two 8'-long 2 x 4s and cut one to 6' 5½" and one to 6' 7". These are the vertical jack studs that will support the header. One will sit on the bottom plate flush with the 7' 1" stud in place, and one will rest on the floor/platform at corner C. Nail these in place (see photo 39).

**51.** Next, lay your tape measure along the top face of the header, and make a mark at 17¼" and another at 18¾" and draw an X between this set of marks for stud placement. Place your 4' level on end on these marks, and transfer these marks to the bottom of the top plate. Draw an X between this set of marks. Measure the distance from the top face of your header to the bottom of the top plate at this stud location. Set your circular saw to an 18½° bevel. Select a 2 x 4 and cut it at this 18½° bevel according to this measurement. Place and nail in the marked stud location (see photo 40). The rough opening for your door is now framed in.

**52.** The next step is to frame in the rest of this wall and the rough opening for the fold-down potting shelf/window. First, measure from the outside of the bottom plate where your rough door opening begins and make marks at 8½", 10", 47⅞", and 49⅜". Transfer these marks to the top of the bottom plate, using your 4' level as a guide. Draw an X between these two sets of marks for stud placement. Set your circular saw to an 18½° bevel, select one 6'-long 2 x 4, and cut it to 5' 10-⅛". (Note: This measurement is the high point of the bevel's slope.) Now select an 8'-long 2 x 4, and cut it to 6' 11¼". Using the stud location marks you've made on the bottom plate, place these studs and use your 4' level to ensure that their placement is plumb. Then, nail the studs to the top and bottom plate. (See photo 41.)

**53.** Reset your circular saw's blade to its normal perpendicular cutting position. Select one 8'-long 2 x 4 and cut two pieces 3' 1⅞" long. These will be the sill and header for the fold-down potting shelf/window. From the top of the bottom plate, measure up on each of the studs you've just secured and make a mark at 25½", 27", 57½", and 59". Transfer the marks to the inside faces of both studs, and draw an X between each set of marks. Nail the header in at the upper stud location, and the sill in at the lower location (see photo 42).

**54.** Measuring from the inside top of the window header, make marks on the bottom face of the header and the top face of the sill at the following inch points: 4⅜", 5⅞", 20⅜", 21⅞", 36⅜", and 37⅞". Mark the same inch points on the top face of the bottom plate. Draw an X between each set of marks. These are stud locations for the remaining vertical wall studs between the header and top plate, and the

**41**

bottom plate and sill. Select one 8'-long 2 x 4 and cut 3 square pieces 25½" long; these are the studs that will be positioned below the window. Nail them in place at the stud locations. Next, set your circular saw to an 18½° bevel. Take one 6'-long 2 x 4 and

cut one 24"-long piece, one 18⅞" piece, and one 13½" piece, all at an 18½° bevel. (These measurements are to the long point of the bevel, or the high point of the bevel's slope). Nail these in place (see photo 43).

■

### SETTING THE ROOF RAFTERS

### (See figs. 8A, 9, and 10, page 113)

Now that your wall framing is complete, you're ready to start building the roof. The first step is to set the rafters, after which you will install wood and felt sheathing in preparation for the metal roofing material.

**55.** First, select six 12'-long 2 x 6s. Cut these to an 18½° angle on one end. Laying your tape measure from the long point of this angle to the other end of the 2 x 6, make a mark at 11' 7⅛". (This mark denotes the short point of the 18½° angle.) Next, set your saw to normal perpendicular cutting position, and cut these ends of the boards at the 11' 7⅛" mark. These are the rafters for the roof.

**42**

**43**

**56.** Two of these rafters will be positioned flush with the outsides and ends of the top plates for wall A-C and D-B. To determine placement locations for the remaining four rafters, measure along the top plates for walls B-A and C-D, marking the following inch points so that they correspond on the two top plates: 23¼", 24¾", 47¼", 4-¾", 71¼", 72¾", 95¼", and 96¾". Starting with the end rafters, position them flush with the ends of the top plates and measure straight out and horizontally from wall B-A until you have a 1' overhang. Secure both rafters by toenailing from the outside of the rafter into the top plate, with nails approximately 24" apart. (See photos 44 and 45.)

**57.** Now that the two end rafters are in place, take a length of string or your chalk line, and run it from the outsides of the ends of the rafters on the B-A side (see photo 46). This will be a guide to indicate placement for the remaining rafters, to make sure their ends are aligned. Next, position the rafters at the placement locations you marked in step 56 and toenail them to the top plates for walls B-A and C-D (see photo 47). Next, install the rafter ties at the points where the rafters meet the insides of the top plates. Use two rafter ties at each end of each rafter. (See photo 48.)

■

### DECKING AND SHEATHING THE ROOF

*Note:* **For this section, you will use standard-sized wood screws and 1¼" roofing tacks as fasteners.**

**58.** Once your rafters are set, you're ready to begin sheathing the roof. Set your circular saw's blade to an 18½° bevel, and select one 12'-long 2 x 6. Cut the length of this 2 x 6 on the groove edge to 11' 10½". Lay the cut 2 x 6 face down with the long point of the beveled edge flush with the end of the rafter on the B-A side (see photo 49). There should be 11¼" overhang at both the wall A-C and wall D-B sides. Secure this board to the roof rafters using wood screws spaced approximately 8" apart. Take twelve 12'-long 2 x 6s and place and secure these as you have secured the first, working up the slope of the

44

45

46

47

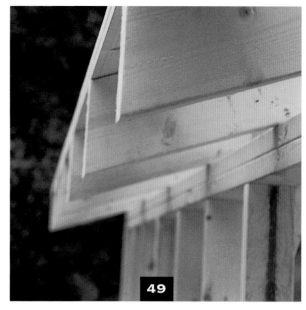

49

48

roof (see photo 50). (There will be approximately a 12" overhang on both sides; you will cut this to length later.) The last 2 x 6 will have to be cut to fit. Cut it at an 18½° bevel on the tongue edge of the board. From the outside face of the top rafter on the C-D side, measure out 11¼" and mark this point. Next, run your chalk line between this mark and the end of the first board you nailed in place and snap the chalk line (see photo 51). Set your circular saw at

a normal perpendicular cutting position, and cut along this line, making the ends of all the decking boards even (see photo 52).

**59.** Now you can install the felt roofing. From your roll of 3'-wide roofing felt, cut one piece approximately 13' long. Lay this piece flush with the roof end at side B-A, and using 1¼" roofing tacks spaced approximately every 6", secure it to the wood decking. Use three or four tacks to secure the felt to the roof ends on both of these sides, and leave a small amount of overhang on both the A-C and D-B sides. (You will trim it to fit once it is fully secured.) Cut another piece of felt the same length, and lay it on the next uncovered section of the roof, overlapping the first piece by approximately 2" (see photo 53). Secure this piece as you secured the first. Continue this pattern, attaching lengths of felt up the slope of the roof until the roof is fully covered. Last, trim the overhang on both sides so that it is flush with the edges of the end decking boards on sides A-C and D-B (see photo 54).

■

### BLOCKING THE RAFTERS

*Note:* **For this section, you will use galvanized 16d nails as fasteners.**

**60.** The next step is to block the rafters so that

**50**

**51**

**52**

**53**

54

55

56

nailed to these blocks. The blocks will be positioned tightly between all rafters on sides B-A and C-D, so that they are aligned with the edges of the top plates on both of these sides. Using your tape measure, measure all the distances between the rafters (you can transfer these measurements to a spare 2 x 4, and use it as a cutting guide). (See photo 55.) These measurements may vary slightly, and the rafters at the ends will be shorter than the intermediate rafters. Since these blocking pieces must be nailed flush with the underside of the sloped roof decking, you will need to cut them at an $18\frac{1}{2}°$ bevel. Set your circular saw accordingly. Select a 10'-long 2 x 4 and cut pieces lengthwise according to the measurements you have taken. Using two nails per side, toenail each piece of blocking to the rafters on either side (see photo 56).

■

## ATTACHING THE SIDING

*Note:* **For this section and through step 67, you will use galvanized 8d nails. All siding should be positioned with the bottom end about 1" below the top of the floor framing, and secured to the framing studs with nails spaced approximately 12" apart.**

### WALL A-C

**61.** Select one 4' x 8' piece of plywood and place it on wall A-C flush with corner C, and use a couple of nails to secure it temporarily. From the inside of the shed, scribe the location of the door opening with a pencil. Remove the plywood, and, using your circular saw set at its normal perpendicular cutting position, cut along the lines you've marked for the door opening. (Set aside this piece of plywood you've just cut out; you will use it to make the door for the shed.) Reposition the siding as before, and secure it. Next, where this siding ends along wall A-C, measure the distance from the floor to the top of the wall; also, measure vertically from the floor to top of the wall at corner A. These measurements indicate the cut line for the top of your next section of siding. Select a second sheet of plywood, and use your tape measure to mark these measurements on the plywood. Snap a chalk line between the two marks, and cut along this line. Now, place the piece of plywood next to the previously installed piece (there will be a ⅜" overlap), and temporarily nail in place. Using the same procedure you used to cut out the door opening, scribe the siding to indicate the rough opening for the fold-out potting shelf/window, and cut accordingly. (Set aside the piece of plywood you've just cut out; you will use it to make the fold-out potting shelf/window.) Reposition and secure the siding as before. (Do not install siding in the small triangular area above the door yet; you will need to install flashing here first.)

### WALL C-D

**62.** Place a sheet of plywood flush with corner C on side C-D, and secure it temporarily. Using a pencil, scribe the locations of the windows from the inside of the shed (see photo 57). Remove the plywood, and, with your circular saw at a normal perpendicular angle, cut out these openings for the windows. Reposition the plywood, and secure it. Select a second sheet of plywood and place it flush with the piece you've just secured, allowing for the ⅜" overlap. Secure this piece temporarily, scribe the openings for the remaining windows, and cut. Select a third sheet of plywood and cut it to 2 x 8. Position it next to the second sheet, and repeat the scribing and cutting processes as per the first sections of siding. You should now have plywood covering approximately the bottom two-thirds of wall C-D, with the windows cut out (see photo 58). (Do not attach siding for the upper portion of this wall yet; you will need to install flashing first.)

### WALL D-B.

**63.** Place one sheet of plywood flush with corner D, and secure it. The section of siding that covers the upper portion of this wall will not be attached until after flashing is installed. Next, where this siding ends, measure from the floor to the top of the wall. Also measure this vertical distance at corner B. Transfer the measurements to another piece of plywood, cut accordingly, and secure. (See photo 59.)

**60**

**61**

**62**

**64.** To attach siding for this wall, you must first scribe and cut spaces to allow for the roof rafters. Select a scrap 2 x 2 at least 10' long, and place it flush with the outside of the rafter at one end of side B-A, directly under the rafters. Using your pencil, make marks on the 2 x 2 indicating the outside locations of all rafters. This marked 2 x 2 will be a guide for transferring spaces for the rafters on to the plywood siding for wall B-A (see photo 60).

**65.** Next, select one sheet of plywood and lay it so that the top is flush with the end of the 2 x 2 where your marks begin. Measure the end of one rafter from top to bottom; this measurement should be approximately 5¾". At each point you've marked on the siding, measure 5¾" (or the distance you have measured) vertically, and use your framing square to mark the plywood accordingly. Connect the dots! And cut along these lines. Last, measure from the bottom of the roof to an inch below the floor framing. This will be the overall length of your siding for this wall. Measure from the top of the piece you have just notched, and cut the plywood to this length. Repeat this process to side the rest of this wall. (You'll need another full 4' x 8', and one 4' x 8' cut to 2' x 8'.)

### INSTALLING FLASHING AND ATTACHING REMAINING SIDING FOR WALLS A-C, D-B, AND C-D

**66.** Before attaching the remaining sections of siding to the upper portions of walls A-C, D-B, and C-D, you'll need to install flashing along the tops of the attached plywood sheets where they will meet the bottoms of the final sections. Measure the width of the siding at these locations, and use your circular saw to cut pieces of flashing to length. Place the flashing so that it fits snugly around the top edge of the plywood, flush with the wall framing, and secure with a small nail or tack so that ½ the nail head overlaps the edge of the flashing (see photo 61). Finish siding these walls by measuring the outside vertical distances of the uncovered portions of wall, as you did in previous steps, and cutting plywood to fit. Refer to steps 62 and 63 to cut out spaces for the rafters on the wall C-D side.

■

### TRIMMING THE WALL CORNERS

The next step is to trim all the corners where walls meet, so that the eight lookouts on wall C-D can be secured to corner trim at corners C and D.

**67.** At each corner, measure from the bottom of the roof to the bottom of the siding; this measurement indicates the length of the trim boards. Since each corner is formed by one 8'-long and one 10'-long wall, you'll need four 10'-long 1 x 4s and four 8'-long 1 x 4s. Setting your circular saw at its normal perpendicular cutting position, cut these boards to length. One board at each corner will need to be notched, to accommodate a roof rafter (refer to steps 62 and 63). Position the 1 x 4s face down flush with the corners, and nail approximately every 6" to secure (see photo 62).

■

### INSTALLING THE LOOKOUTS

The six boards attached in a diagonal pattern to the rafters and walls are called "lookouts." While they provide some additional support for the existing structure, they are mostly decorative—great for hanging your favorite plants from!

**68.** Select two 12'-long spruce 2 x 4s. Set your circular saw to a 45° angle, and cut six 3'-long boards. Place one cut board on edge with the angled end flush with the wall, and the other end against a rafter. Move the 2 x 4 up and down until the lower end of the rafter is flush with the bottom face of the 2 x 4. With your pencil, mark a line across the face of the board where the rafter and 2 x 4 meet. Set your circular saw to its normal perpendicular cutting position, and cut the board along this line. Use this 2 x 4 to transfer the cut line to the remaining five 2 x 4s. Using two or three siding nails at the end of

each 2 x 4, secure them to wall C-D and the rafters (see photo 63).

■

### ATTACHING THE FASCIA

Next you will install fascia, the trim around the perimeter of the roof.

**69.** Select four 12'-long 1 x 8s, and set your saw to its normal perpendicular cutting position. For sides B-A and C-D, cut two 1 x 8s to 11' 10-½". Position these so that the top of the fascia is flush with the top of the roof's edge, and secure (see photo 64). Now position and temporarily secure the remaining two 1 x 8s flush with the top of the roof on sides A-C and D-B. Use your speed or framing square to

64

65

66

mark the ends where these boards meet the already installed fascia, cut to length, reposition, and secure.

## INSTALLING THE VENTS

*Note:* **For this section, you will use ¹⁄₂" wood screws as fasteners.**

**70.** Centering the location for each vent between rafters and above the top plate of wall C-D, use a framing square to mark a 3" x 15" opening. (Since the vents will be attached to the outside of the wall, the openings will be slightly smaller than the vents themselves.) Using a compass saw or jigsaw, cut out these openings (see photo 65). Center the vents over these openings, and secure. Repeat this process to install the vents for wall A-B. (See photo 66.)

■

## INSTALLING EXTERIOR TRIM FOR WALL C-D WINDOWS

*Note:* **For this section, you will use 8d siding nails as fasteners.**

**71.** Select two 8'-long cedar 1 x 4s. Lay both boards down on a work surface, measure 1³⁄₄" in on the face of each board at both ends, and mark these points. Snap the chalk line between the two points and cut along this line; you'll now have four 8'-long 1 x 2s. Lay your speed square on the face of one of these 1 x 2s at the end of the board, and mark the 45° angle (the windows are 15¹⁄₂" x 15¹⁄₂"). Set your circular saw to its normal perpendicular cutting position, and cut this line. Next, measure from the long point of this angle to 18¹⁄₄". Mark this point, which will be the long point of the 45° angle at this end of the board, then use your speed square to mark the angle on the board and cut. Repeat this process four times, position these boards flush with the perimeter of the window opening, and use three nails per piece of trim to secure (see photo 67). You will see approximately ³⁄₈" overhang when looking at the window from the inside; this is called the "reveal," and will serve as a rest or stop for the window glass. Repeat this process to trim the remaining four windows.

## Installing Glass And Interior Trim For The Wall C-D Windows

*Note:* **For this section, you will use 6d siding nails as fasteners.**

**72.** From a 4' x 4' sheet of Plexiglass, cut five pieces 15¼" square. (You will have enough left over for the door window.) To "cut" the Plexiglass, use your framing square or level and utility knife: Measure the dimensions on the Plexiglass and mark, then score these lines a couple of times, and break the Plexiglass. From the inside of the shed, fit the Plexiglass squares in the window openings so that they fit tightly against the exterior trim's reveal.

**73.** To secure the Plexiglass, you will need to install "stops," or a small trim, around the Plexiglass' perimeter on the interior wall. First, select one 8'-long 2 x 4 and measure in ⅜" on the face of the board at both ends. Cut the board accordingly; you will now have a ⅜" x 1½" x 8' board. Repeat this process so that you have three boards this size. (See photo 68.)

**74.** From one of these boards, cut two 15½"-long pieces to trim the top and bottom of the window, and two 14¾"-long pieces to trim the sides. Position these around the perimeter of the glass, and secure to the window framing (See photo 68.) Repeat this process to trim the remaining four windows.

## Making, Trimming, And Installing The Door For Wall A-C

*Note:* **For steps in this and the following section, you will 1⅝" wood screws, 8dsiding nails, and 1½"-long ⁵⁄₁₆"-diameter lag bolts as fasteners.**

**75.** First, select the piece of plywood you cut and set aside in step 60 (the door); one 14'-long 2 x 4; and one 12'-long 2 x 4. These 2 x 4s will be used to frame the perimeter of the inside of the door. Cut

the 14'-long 2 x 4 into two 7' boards. Lay one 7'-long 2 x 4 flush with one side and one end of the plywood door. Mark it where it meets the other end of the plywood door, and cut any excess. Cut the other 7'-long 2 x 4 to the same length, and secure from the outside of the door. Measure the distance between these secured framing boards at the top and bottom of the door, cut the remaining 2 x 4 to fit flush with the vertical boards, then position and secure the horizontal framing boards. The remaining piece of 2 x 4 will serve as a diagonal framing board. Place it diagonally between the top of one vertical framing board and the bottom of the other, and secure to the framing boards (see photo 69).

69

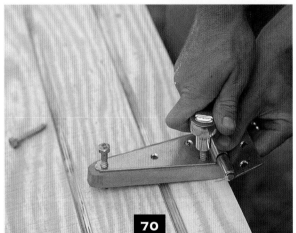
70

71

**76.** To trim the door opening, begin by selecting one 10'-long 1 x 4. Measure from the edge of the corner trim on corner C to 3½" past the far corner of the door opening, and cut the 1 x 4 to this length. Position this board so that the bottom of the trim is flush with the door opening, and nail in place. Next, on the left side of the door opening, measure from the bottom of the siding to the bottom of the piece of horizontal trim you have just installed. Cut a piece of 1 x 4 to this length, and secure it.

**77.** The next step is to position and hang the door. Select a scrap piece of cedar, and nail it to the door where the hinges will be positioned, approximately 8" down from the top and up from the bottom of the door. This piece of cedar will serve as a spacer to ensure that the hinges meet the corner trim to which they will be attached. Next, attach the hinges to the door at the same locations. (The pivot point of the hinge should be flush with the outside edge of the door. Note: To avoid splintering the cedar, predrill ¼" holes for the lag screws.) (See photo 70.) Position the door in the opening and use scrap pieces of lumber to shim the door so it is centered (see photo 71). Scribe the locations where the hinges rest on the cedar trim, and predrill holes in these locations. Install the lag bolts using a ratchet and socket, and remove the wood shims.

**78.** Last, centering the window in the top section of the door, follow the procedures you used in steps 60 and 67 to trim and install the glass for this window.

■

### MAKING, TRIMMING, AND INSTALLING THE FOLD-OUT POTTING SHELF/ WINDOW FOR WALL A-C

*Note:* **For this section, you will use a length of chain, in addition to the above-mentioned fasteners, to attach the fold-out potting shelf/window to the window framing.**

**79.** Select one 8'-long 1 x 4, and cut it lengthwise down the middle, as you did in step 67; using these boards, follow the same procedure you used in step 69 to trim the windows on wall C-D, trim the exterior opening for the fold-out potting shelf /window. Next, use wood screws to attach two hinges to the sill plate where it meets the trim, so that the hinges pivot down (see photo 72). (The trim will need to be notched at the hinge locations; a rough notch the length of the hinge base made with a utility knife or chisel will work fine.) Select the piece of plywood you cut and set aside in step 59, and, referring again to step 69, frame the perimeter of the fold-out potting shelf/window on the shed's interior.

**80.** Using scrap pieces of lumber as shims, position and center the fold-out potting shelf, and use wood screws to attach the hinges to the potting shelf (see photo 73). Next, fold the secured potting shelf out. Use your 4' level to ensure that the shelf is level, then stretch a piece of chain from the outside corners of the potting shelf to the inside of the window frame, and secure with wood or lag screws (See photo 74).

### INSTALLING THE METAL ROOFING

The last step in finishing construction on your shed is to install the metal roofing.

**81.** Installation for different types and even brands of metal roofing vary, so you will need to follow procedures specified by the manufacturer regarding the number of screws used and their spacing. The rest is simple—lay your presized 12' x 11' 10½¨ metal roofing and position it squarely on top of the decking boards and felt sheathing.

**82.** Hurrah! You're at the finish line! Paint or stain your shed with the hues and tints you prefer. Then open a bottle of your favorite libation, take a swig, and do a dance of thanks to the construction deities!

72

73

74

A little design ingenuity can turn a basic 8' x 10' structure with a shed roof like our Potting Shed into all kinds of interesting backyard storage and recreational buildings. By slightly varying the conventional shed roofline, using different materials and techniques for roofing and siding, and changing door and window types and placements, the Potting Shed can be transformed into multi-use structures for organizing and safeguarding tools and equipment, working, or just relaxing and having fun.

In this section, you'll find renderings for four variations in styles ranging from classical to modern, no-frills to fanciful. The basic techniques and processes needed to build these sheds are the same as those used to build the Potting Shed, and we've provided you with lists of any materials and tools you'll need in addition to those described in Chapters Three and Four. (Additional tools and materials lists, along with architectural plans for the variations, are in the plans section at the back of the book.) Building some of the variations will also require using techniques novices may not be familiar with, so if you're a newcomer to backyard carpentry, you'll need to pick up a good book that discusses the appropriate specific techniques.

### DUAL-USE STORAGE SHED (SH-2)

**W**ith its clean, unassuming lines and traditional board and batten siding, this dual-purpose storage shed is at home in just about any landscape, in just about any region. (It's also great for those of us who like our organizing organized for us!) Its neatly divided interior and multiple entryways make it perfect for dual use. You can easily store an assortment of small-to-medium-sized gardening implements and accessories on one side, and use the open side with arched entryways for stacking and storing firewood, keeping bikes out of the rain, or stashing bags of mulch, gravel, and other landscaping ingredients.

*For plans, see figs. 17-30, pages 115-118.*

### FRENCH PAVILION (SH-3)

**I**t's not hard to imagine this elegant little pavilion taking on any one of a number of different duties. Its neat proportions and mix of formal French doors and inviting latticework make it ideal as a debonair accent for a private formal garden, a lovely open-air pool cabana or changing room, or—fitted out with a couple of comfortable outdoor chairs and a low table—a delightful little summer room in which to chat and sip lemonade, meander through chapters of a good book, or simply while away the hours listening to birdsong or watching afternoon shift its hues to the rose and periwinkle and indigo of dusk. The lattice sides and low shelf for potted flowers or plants offer all kinds of opportunities for decorating with your favorite flora. A great setting for kids' tea parties and make-believe games, too!

*For plans, see figs. 31-42, pages 119-122.*

## CONTEMPORARY HOLD-ALL (SH-4)

This fun structure puts a new twist on the boring-old-utility-building theme. By choosing metal siding in one of the many bright colors available, and topping this shed off with a vaulted canvas roof and translucent end panels, you can turn what might have been a homely storage shed into a contemporary focal point in your yard or garden. Its single door makes this shed better for storing the smaller gardening standards up to the push-mower scale. Or choose an all-translucent roof, and let it work as a greenhouse for you!

*For plans, see figs. 43-53, pages 123-126.*

## CLASSIC ALL-PURPOSE STORAGE SHED (SH-5)

Tidy clapboard siding and handsome French doors give this version of an all-purpose storage shed a slightly more sophisticated appeal, while still providing sensible, no-frills space to protect all manner of gardening and recreational paraphernalia from the elements. With louvre vents installed on two sides, you can also keep the doors open in gentle weather, move a small potting table in, and get your fingers in the soil.

*For plans, see figs. 54-66, pages 127-130*

# CHAPTER SIX

# THE GABLE-ROOFED STORAGE SHED AND SIX VARIATIONS

## THE STORAGE SHED

In Chapter Five, we gave you detailed, step-by-step instructions to build our Potting Shed, an 8' x 10' shed with a shed roof, and additional information necessary to complete four sheds whose structures are variations on the Potting Shed's simple shape. On the following pages, a materials list, exploded-view drawing, and how-to instructions will lead you through construction for our Storage Shed, another simple 8' x 10', this time with a traditional gable roof. Again, we wanted to offer you lots of choices. So, along with information for the Storage Shed, this chapter provides renderings for six variations on its simple lines, in a span of interesting designs to satisfy numerous tastes and requirements.

Written building instructions for the Storage Shed are not as particularized as those for the Potting Shed, though visual aids—plans and the exploded-view drawing—keep the project straightforward and manageable. ( For architecural plans for the Storage Shed, see figs. 67 - 81, pages 132-135.)

Accomplished weekend carpenters and even perennial do-it-yourselfers will find its construction easy to handle. Beginners who decide to tackle the Storage Shed will find it helpful to refer to parallel steps in instructions for the Potting Shed, to complete certain phases in construction. (Because of their different rooflines and door and window locations, processes for building the Potting Shed and Storage Shed differ, but share identical construction principles.) Like the variations in Chapter Five, the variations in this chapter do involve some additional techniques not covered in this book. But, well-armed with these variations' illustrations, plans and additional materials lists, it will be easy to gather the extra information necessary at your local library, or by talking to a builder or building supplier in your area.

# MATERIALS AND SUPPLIES

## LUMBER

| DESCRIPTION | QTY. | MATERIAL | DIMENSIONS |
|---|---|---|---|
| Batter boards | 5 | 1 x 4s (any type) | 12' long |
| Base | 2 | pressure-treated pine 4 x 6s | 8' long |
| | 2 | pressure-treated pine 4 x 6s | 10' long |
| Floor | 7 | pressure-treated pine 2 x 6s | 8' long |
| | 1 | pressure-treated pine 2 x 6 | 10' long |
| | 3 | ½" CDX plywood | 4' x 8' |
| Wall framing | 6 | pine 2 x 4s | 10' long |
| | 31 | pine 2 x 4s | 8' long |
| Rafters | 12 | pine 2 x 6s | 10' long |
| Roof | 20 | tongue-and-groove cedar 2 x 6s | 12' long |
| | 2 | copper drip | 12' long |
| (Ridge cap) | 2 | cedar 1 x 6s | 12' long |
| Siding | 10 | ½" T1-11 plywood | 4' x 8' |
| | 250 sq. ft | cedar clapboards | 5½" x 10' |
| | 14 | ½" cedar trim boards | 4" x 8' |
| Door | 1 | ½" CDX plywood | 4' x 8' |
| | 6 | tongue-and-groove cedar | 4" x 8' |

## OTHER

| DESCRIPTION | QTY. | MATERIAL | DIMENSIONS |
|---|---|---|---|
| Batter boards | 1 | mason's line | |
| Foundation | 6 | cylindrical cardboard forms | 8" diameter |
| | 12 | bags premixed concrete | 40# |
| | 1 | bag gravel | 40# |
| Roof | 100' | felt roll-roofing | 3' wide |
| | 2 | presized metal roofing | 8' 6" |
| Siding | 2 | copper drip | |
| Vents | 2 | round metal vents | 1' diameter |
| Windows | 1 | Plexiglass sheet | 2' x 2' |

## FASTENERS

- 1 box 1½" drywall screws

- 10 boxes 2" galvanized 16d nails

- 14 standard-size joist hangers

- 1 box joist hanger nails

- 10 4" x 4" adjustable post anchors

- 10 ½" x 6" galvanized anchor bolts with nuts

- 12 3 ⁹⁄₁₆" x 1½" metal variable pitch connectors

- 1 box 1¼" roofing tacks

- 6 boxes galvanized 8d siding nails

- 1 box galvanized 6d siding nails

- 1 box ½" wood screws

- 1 box 1⅝" wood screws

- 6 hinges

- 6 1½" ⁵⁄₁₆" diameter lag bolts

## LAYING OUT YOUR SHED;
## PREPPING THE CONCRETE PIERS;
## POURING THE CONCRETE PIERS;
## FRAMING THE BASE;
## AND FRAMING AND DECKING THE FLOOR

Before you begin to build the walls of the Storage Shed, you will need to complete the phases of construction listed above. The processes for these phases for this shed are identical to those used for the Potting Shed in Chapter Five. To complete these phases of the building project, follow steps 1–33 in Chapter Five (see pages 55-62).

## FRAMING WALL A-C

**(See fig.75)**

*Note*: **To frame this and the other three walls, you will need to refer to corresponding framing drawings to determine the dimensions of various studs and other framing members. For steps 1–22, you will use galvanized 2" 16d nails as fasteners, unless otherwise specified.**

**1.** Select one 8'-long 2 x 4; this will be the bottom plate (the horizontal board at the bottom of the wall ) for wall A-C. Cut this 2 x 4 to the dimension indicated on fig.75. Lay it on a your built shed floor or other level work platform.

**2.** Using a tape measure, make a series of marks from left to right on the bottom plate to match the dimensions on fig. 75. These marks represent centers for placement of the vertical studs for this wall. On either side of these marks, measure ¾" and make additional marks at these locations. For the end stud at either end of the wall, measure in 1-½" from each end of the bottom plate. Using a framing square, mark a line perfectly perpendicular to the sides of the bottom plate at these marks. Draw an X between each set of marks; these Xs indicate exact locations for placement of the vertical wall studs.

**3.** Taking dimensions from fig. 75, select appropriate lengths of lumber and cut the vertical studs with a circular saw to the necessary lengths and angles; use a speed square as a guide to make accurate cuts with your circular saw. (*Note:* This shed has a 12:12 pitch roof, so all cuts to the ends of the vertical studs that meet the top plate are at 45° angles. All dimensions of 2 x 4 studs with angled ends are to the long end of the cut.) Once cut, lay the studs out with the bottom plate on a flat surface, in the arrangement shown in fig. 75.

**4.** Once you have cut all the studs for this wall, select another 8'-long 2 x 4, and make marks on this board duplicating the X marks you made on the bottom plate. Set this board aside for now; it will serve as a stud guide for the vertical studs.

**5.** Next, use a speed or framing square to transfer the X marks for stud locations on to the edge of the bottom plate. Place the vertical studs perpendicular to the bottom plate and position them over the X marks. Secure these to the bottom plate with a couple of nails at each stud location.

**6.** Measure 5' up from the bottom plate at each vertical side of the wall. Take the stud guide you marked in step 5, and place the stud guide with the bottom of the board aligned with the 5' mark, on top of the vertical studs. Make sure the left end of the stud guide is aligned with the left end of the bottom plate, and that the markings on the stud guide are face down. When the stud guide is properly placed, align the vertical studs with the X marks, and use a single nail at each stud to temporarily secure the stud guide to the vertical studs. Leave the nail head approximately $\frac{1}{4}$" above the surface of the stud guide, to ease nail removal later. (*Note:* This stud guide is used to ensure that the studs are parallel to each other, and vertically plumb.)

**7.** Taking dimensions from fig.75, select appropriate lengths of lumber and cut the remaining horizontal studs, and two top plates. Place the horizontal studs in position and secure with two nails at each connection.

**8.** Last, nail the top plates to the vertical studs using two nails per stud.

**9.** Remove the stud guide and set this wall aside.

### FRAMING WALL D-B

**(See fig. 78)**

Since they are both "gable-end" walls, the process for framing wall D-B is the same as for framing wall A-C, substituting fig.78 for fig.75.

**10.** To frame wall D-B, follow steps 1 - 9 listed above in Framing Wall A-C, using the dimensions shown in fig.78.

### FRAMING WALL B-A

**(See fig.76)**

*Note:* **Because there are no windows or doors in walls B-A and C-D, the processes for building these two walls are exactly the same.**

**11.** Select three 10'-long 2 x 4s; these will be the bottom and doubled top plate for wall B-A. Lay the

bottom plate on edge on your work platform, and one of the top plates on edge, parallel and about 6' away from the bottom plate.

**12.** As you did for the two gable-end walls, use a tape measure to make a series of marks from left to right on one face of the bottom plate, according to the dimensions in fig. 76. Duplicate this set of marks on one face of one of the top plates. Measure $\frac{3}{4}$" on each side and make additional marks at these locations, and draw an X between each set of marks. The Xs indicate locations for placement of vertical studs for this wall. Taking dimensions from fig.78, select appropriate lengths of lumber and cut the vertical studs to length (the lengths of all of these studs will be identical).

**13.** Once the studs are cut, place them in the locations you have marked. Use your framing square to ensure that all the studs are plumb, then secure them to the marked top and bottom plate with two nails at each connection. Last, secure the second top plate to the first, and set this wall aside.

### FRAMING WALL C-D

**(See fig.77)**

**14.** To frame wall C-D, follow steps 11-13, substituting fig.77 for fig. 76.

### RAISING WALLS A-C, B-A, D-B, AND C-D

*Note:* **To raise the walls, you will want to recruit some friends to help—the more the better, but you'll need at least two or three extra pairs of hands.**

**15.** Drive two stakes (reuse those you sharpened for the batter boards used to lay out your shed) in the ground, about 8' apart, parallel to and approximately 5' away from side A-C of the base/floor structure.

**16.** Place wall A-C on the platform, aligning the sides of the wall's bottom plate with the sides of the base. Carefully lean the wall up into position, perpendicular to the base.

**17.** Attach an 8'-long 2 x 4 to each of the stakes, and diagonally raise them to meet wall A-C. Attach these 2 x 4s, which will serve as temporary braces, to the inside faces of the two outside wall studs. Use screws to temporarily secure these braces, to allow for adjustment to make sure the wall's raised position is plumb.

**18.** Next, secure the bottom plate to the base with two nails at 16" on center. Use your 4' level to ensure that the wall's position is plumb.

**19.** Once wall A-C is plumb and level, repeat steps 16–19 to raise wall C-D.

**20.** Secure wall A-C to wall C-D by nailing through the corner and additional vertical studs at corner C (see fig. 80). Make sure that the outside corners of these two walls are aligned.

**21.** Repeat steps 15–20 to raise walls D-B and B-A, and secure them to walls C-D and A-C.

### Framing The Rafters

**(Refer to fig.79 for rafter layout. See figs. 72, 73, and 74 for additional information)**

*Note:* For steps 32–33, you will use 3½" galvanized 12d nails as fasteners.

**22.** First, select four 10'-long 2 x 6s. These will be used to construct one rafter. (*Note:* Each side of the peak will consist of two glued and nailed 2 x 6s with ½" plywood spacers between them. See figs. 72, 73, and 74.)

**23.** Each rafter will require six spacers. To make the spacers, cut 36 ½" plywood strips to 5½" x 8'. You will also need to cut a total of six spacers for the peak (See fig.73 for the dimensions of these spacers; refer to fig.79 for overall spacer locations.) Set these aside for now.

**24.** Next, cut six 5' 1"-long 2 x 4s to create horizontal collar ties, as shown on fig. 79. (Note: The dimension is taken from the long ends of the ties,

and the ends are cut at a 45° angle.) Set these aside for now.

**25.** Select 24 10'-long 2 x 6s, and cut the rafters to the dimensions specified in fig. 79. (Note: To make this go smoothly, cut one rafter to the proper dimensions and use it as a pattern for the remaining rafters. This will ensure that all rafters are the same, and you won't have to measure 24 rafters!) Use a speed square as a guide to make accurate cuts; since this is a 12:12 pitch roof, all cuts at the top and bottom of rafters are at 45°. ( See figs. 73 and 74.)

**26.** Lay two 8' 5⅞"-long 2 x 6s on your working platform to create the gable shape shown in fig.79. Apply a generous bead of wood glue on one side of each of the spacers you made in step 17, and place them on the two rafters at the positions shown on drawing 19. Apply glue to all the spacers, and place the remaining rafters on top of the spacers, precisely aligning them with the first two rafters' positions.

**27.** Check all dimensions, and attach the collar ties in position as shown on fig.79.

**28.** Once you have ensured that all your dimensions are accurate, use five nails at each spacer location to secure the top rafters to the bottom ones.

**29.** Repeat steps 20–22, to create a total of six gable roof rafters.

**30.** On each rafter, measure 4' down from the peak on both sides and make marks at these points on the tops of the rafters. Set these aside.

### Setting The Rafters

Now that your rafters are constructed, you're ready to set them in position, attached to walls B-A and C-D. Keep the folks close by who helped you raise the shed walls! You'll need them to help set the rafters.

**31.** Begin by placing metal variable pitch connectors on the tops of the doubled top plates on walls

B-A and C-D, in the positions indicated on figs. 76 and 77. Install these at all 12 locations (see fig. 72).

**32.** Next, select two 12'-long 2 x 4s, and mark these boards from left to right 2' on center. You will use these to keep the rafters in their correct positions until the tongue-and-groove wood roof decking is installed.

**33.** Take one rafter section and place it flush with wall D-B. Place the bottom of the rafter into the variable pitch connector. Measure the overhang on each side (this dimension should be 2'; see fig. 78). Once the rafter is correctly positioned, secure the rafter by nailing into it through holes in the metal connector. Then, toenail the rafter to the top plate at 1' 4" intervals.

**34.** Position the next rafter section into its variable pitch connector. Again, the overhang on each side should measure 2'. Note: This rafter will have to be held in place until the next two steps are completed.

**35.** Place one of the 10'-long 2 x 4s that you marked and set aside in step 32 on top of both rafters on the slope closest to wall B-A. Use the marks you made on the top of the rafters to align the 2 x 4 across the rafters. Align the end of the 2 x 4 with the left-hand face of the first rafter. The second rafter should be centered on the 2' mark just to the right; nail at this point. This 2 x 4 will brace the rafters until the roof decking is installed. ( See fig. 76.)

**36.** Using the other 10'-long 2 x 4 you marked in step 32, repeat this process on the C-D side.

**37.** Install the remaining rafters using the process you used in step 33, positioning the rafters in their appropriate locations.

## DECKING AND SHEATHING THE ROOF; INSTALLING THE METAL ROOFING

*Note*: **For this section, you will use ½" wood screws, 1¼" roofing tacks, construction glue, and metal roofing screws as fasteners.**

**38.** To install the tongue-and-groove wood decking, felt roll-roofing, and metal roofing, refer to steps 58–59 Sheathing And Decking the Roof, pages 71-72) and 79 (Installing The Metal Roofing, page 81) in Chapter Five, substituting dimensions from figs. 71–79, for the Storage Shed.

## ATTACHING SIDING TO WALLS A-C, B-A, D-B, AND C-D

*Note*: **Cedar clapboard siding, over a layer of plywood siding, is specified for this shed. If you choose, though, you can install the plywood siding and paint or stain it as finished siding.**

**39.** To install plywood siding for all walls, refer to steps 60–66 (Attaching The Siding, pages 74-77) in Chapter Five. If you prefer the specified cedar clapboard siding for the finished look, cut clapboards to length, and install them, overlapping the boards as per the manufacturer's instructions (overlap varies from manufacturer to manufacturer). When securing the clapboards, make sure that you nail them through the plywood underlay into the wall studs.

## INSTALLING TRIM, FASCIA, LOOKOUTS, AND WINDOW; MAKING AND HANGING DOORS; INSTALLING VENTS AND HARDWARE

**40.** Adapt the processes in steps 67-78 and 81 (pages 77-81) in Chapter Five to the dimensions in figs. 75 and 76 to complete these phases of construction.

**41.** Paint or stain your finished Storage Shed, and sit back and admire your work!

# Six Variations On A Simple Structure

While an elementary structure such as our Storage Shed takes care of no-nonsense storage needs, it's fun to have options that are imaginative but still do the job. In this section, we've offered seven sheds which are all variations on the Storage Shed's gable roofline and 8' x 10' structure.

Additional tools and materials required to build these variations are listed with the plans for each variation. We've specified certain types of woods, mostly cedar, for the variations, but you may choose to substitute other types of lumber to achieve different textures and looks, or to lower overall materials costs.

## Mini-Shed With Canopied Porch (GR-2)

This quaint little building provides compact storage space for small gardening or other tools and supplies, and doubles as an open-air nook for sitting and ... watching the world go by. The more practical-minded might use the sheltered front porch for stacking firewood—or set out a little potting bench, and it makes an ideal area for potting on nice days. With its posts and lattice canopy, you can arrange favorite plants in pretty pots on the porch, trail a favorite flowering vine up the posts and along the roof, and just enjoy the view!

*For plans, see figs. 82–93, pages 136-139*

## Edge-Of-The-Woods Shed (GR-3)

From either approach, this well-designed structure has a clean-cut, bucolic appeal. Divided into two distinct areas, it offers both conventional shed storage space on one side and an inviting screened porch on the other. Perfect for homeowners with minimal storage requirements who want to make the most of a single structure, its screened section can serve as a sitting or reading area in temperate weather, a space to tinker with pots, soil, and seeds, or an all-their-own play area for children.

*For plans, see figs. 94–106, pages 140-143*

## MINIATURE GREEK REVIVAL LODGE (GR-4)

**S**tately columns and classic moulding help this structure give a whole new meaning to the word "shed." Well-proportioned and urbane, it adds polish to any landscape or garden, and makes a wonderful garden storage building, small studio, playhouse, or poolhouse. To soften its look, wind wisteria up around the six pilasters. Then ease back into your favorite garden chair, and call for music and wine!

*For plans, see figs. 107–117, pages 144-147.*

## COOL CANVAS CABANA (GR-5)

**L**ike many of our shed variations, this one-of-a-kind shelter can fill the bill for a number of different functions. Its distinctly casual flair, though, makes it a great choice for a poolside retreat, changing room, or storeroom. Sheathed and roofed in canvas, with fun roll-up Roman screens, it can't help but provide an ideal architectural accent to a recreation and relaxation area. Keep the screens down for storage, or open them all up, and get out of the sun with a good novel or magazine, and a tall glass of iced tea!

*For plans, see figs. 118–128, pages 148-150.*

## PLEIN-AIR SUMMER ROOM (GR-6)

**W**ho hasn't longed for a cozy little getaway at the end of the garden? It's hard not to imagine this comfortable summerhouse tucked away amidst blossoming greenery, with jewel-bright butterflies wheeling and alighting under a golden sun. Its screened sides, ends, and door seem to lure gentle breezes in, making it a great hideaway from summer heat and insects—an excellent choice for those looking for a place to have tea parties for grown-ups or kids, or to simply take time out from the daily grind.

*For plans, see figs. 129-140, pages 151-154.*

## TINY STONE COTTAGE (GR-7)

**R**ustic stone veneer and an arched fairy-tale doorway give this wee building an air of romance and history, while its open interior renders it spacious enough to harbor a large assortment of hand tools, small machines, and other necessary contraptions for garden and grounds.

It's a picturesque alternative for those who need a sturdy storage space but don't want to sacrifice aesthetics to function—as sun, showers, and wind burnish the stone, this shed will become even more alluring over time.

*For plans, see figs. 141–151, pages 155-158.*

# SHED MAKEOVERS

## DECORATING KITS AND OLD SHEDS

**B**uilding a shed of one's own can be fun and rewarding, but let's face it—for some us, the appeal ends abruptly right about at the point where picking up the hammer begins. For others, jam-packed daily schedules make recreation hours precious. You'd rather take a walk, curl up with a good book, or spend time with family and friends, than sweat and haul lumber!

What, then, are the options for owning an attractive, inexpensive shed? You can hire a builder to do the job for you, but that can be costly. Most homeowners turn to the realm of ready-to-assemble kit sheds, which are reasonably priced, easy to put together, and extremely practical.

Kit sheds can be bought from local businesses specializing in back yard storage buildings, most home improvement centers, or mail-ordered through companies that make them. Most kit sheds are small (8' x 10' or 10' x 12'), made of either metal or wood, and come in a limited scope of styles. The less expensive models

are usually unembellished rectangular structures with gable or gambrel roofs and a single door; higher-end versions come in a wider range of shapes and sizes, with windows and sometimes additional doors, along with nicer trims and hardware. A few companies go the distance, creating ready-to-assemble sheds that look as though you *did* build them yourself: sheds with interesting rooflines and distinctive architectural details and accoutrements like cupolas and window boxes, octagonal cabanas with lots of windows, playhouses with turrets and window seats.

While kits certainly have their "pros" (economy! pragmatism!), they also have at least one inescapable "con." At their best, assembled kit sheds tend to look a bit homogenous and boring (how many faux Dutch barns can one neighborhood take?)—at their worst, downright ugly. So we've come up with some easy designs for sprucing up kit sheds to give them different or personalized looks, without spending a lot of effort or money. Since there isn't much beyond painting that can drastically change the appearance of a metal shed, the following ten decorating ideas are designed for sheds made of wood. We've created them with kit sheds in mind, but they could just as easily be adapted for old sheds, or even a shed you build yourself. Or, if you are a more experienced builder, you may want to use the illustrations that follow purely as inspiration to devise plans for a construction project of your own.

## MEDITERRANEAN MINI-VILLA

Whether you've seen a Greek or Italian seaside village first hand, on a postcard, or in a movie, the image of a hillside phalanx of whitewashed villas, their red tile roofs glowing in the sun above the Mediterranean's luminous, otherworldly blue, is not quickly forgotten. It can be fun to turn a little backyard building into an exotic eye-catcher, and if a little Mediterranean flavor appeals to you, the transformation can be pretty easy. It's possible to affix actual red clay tiles to an existing kit-shed roof, but, luckily, several manufacturers make aluminum and steel roofing that simulates clay tiles, and can be even more easily installed. (If you have lots of old terra-cotta

pots around, you could also get creative and break these up to give the effect of red tile roofing.) Whitewash the walls of your shed, or paint them another suitable color, and outline the base, door, window and other areas with lightweight tiles. We've chosen tiles in a bright, deep blue hue, with red accent tiles to match the roof tiles. Given the vast array of tile materials, designs, and colors, you can play with color schemes and tile placement to get the look you prefer. Set a couple of terra cotta urns in the yard or below the windows, and plant them with mint or Bougainvillea or, if the climate is right, some lemon or olive trees!

# ARTS AND CRAFTS BUNGALOW

**A**rchitecture, furniture, and designs from the Arts and Crafts movement, which thrived in Europe and America from the late 1800s through the 1920s, are enjoying a revived heyday. Sadly, no kit is likely to incorporate Arts and Crafts joinery methods, or probably even the movement's signature woods like white or red oak, ash, elm, mahogany, and cherry. Yet by choosing and applying semi-transparent or opaque stains in certain hues, you can give pine, cedar, or other woods used more commonly today a more antique, burnished look. If you're lucky, you may be able to purchase a shed which has a gable roof extended in the front and back, creating eaves (if not, you may have to figure out the easiest way to extend or replace the roof of the particular shed you're working with). Either way, using smallish sections of rough-hewn, quarter-sawn wood to trim the corners of the shed, the windows and door(s), and to install small lookouts and other architectural details as

shown will begin to give the shed the look of the period. For a more thorough Arts and Crafts look, replace existing windows and door(s) with "the real thing"—hunt down leaded windows or doors with spindle treatment trim (you'll probably have to adapt door and window openings). As is often the case, the really fun part is in the details: hardware and decorative additions. Hand-hammered copper pulls used for door handles, with window latches in the same style and material will give an authentic look (there are a number of reproduction hardware companies which make pieces like these). Or peruse a good book on Arts and Crafts techniques, materials, styles, and motifs, and choose pieces which most appeal to you. If you really get on a roll, buy some reproductions William Morris fabric, and hang curtains! Or use the patterns to make your own stencils. Don't get too carried away, though—the philosophy of Arts and Crafts, after all, was "beauty and *simplicity*! "

# FAR EAST PAVILION

If you're partial to Asian elements of style and your landscape or garden reflects those inclinations, you may want to metamorphose your shed's look accordingly. (Since Japanese architectural styles are famously pared down and simple, start out with the least embellished shed you can find!) Unless you're feeling particularly industrious and embark on building on a typical Japanese pagoda roof, you'll probably have to forego that element. But the rest is fairly simple. Just devise a system and design for attaching lengths of bamboo in patterns on the walls of the shed (standard nails or screws should work well), purchase or pick enough bamboo to do the job, and go to work. Using different patterns of

bamboo on different sections of the shed will add texture and visual interest. You can also trim corners, windows and doors with bamboo or other wood, replicating Japanese modes and motifs. If bamboo doesn't grow in your area, you can most likely purchase some at a good all-purpose nursery. There are also a number of mail-order companies that stock many types of bamboo specifically for landscaping projects, and make and sell a range of bamboo garden accessories such as pergolas, trellises, and privacy screens. Some such outfits also carry related Japanese garden accessories—Japanese lanterns, carved or cast Buddhas, and the like—if you really want to go for it.

# ENGLISH POTTING SHED

With a trip to your local home improvement center and a handful of weekend hours to spend, it's easy to turn a bland ready-to-assemble shed into a charming back yard structure for work and storage. The shed's color is up to you ( you may be able to purchase one whose finish suits you, or opt to paint or stain it yourself), though a darkish green or red will look good and weather well. Decide where lattice might look best, and whether you prefer criss-cross or square lattice, and purchase the appropriate number of sheets. (Square lattice is a little harder to find, and tends to be slightly more expensive). Attach sheets of lattice as you see fit, and strategically plant your favorite flowering vine or greenery to trail and weave through the lattice. We've added scalloped fascia to the front and sides for an extra-picturesque look, and filled the window boxes with flora straight from the English country garden.

## VICTORIAN COTTAGE

The Victorian age, which spanned nearly 75 percent of the nineteenth century, left a legacy of architectural and decorative styles the popularity of which seem only to increase over time. The result is that architectural accoutrements and details in Victorian style—originals and replicas—are fairly widely available and easy to find. Depending on how elaborate you choose to get and how much money you want to spend, going Victorian with your shed can be quite simple. Most big home improvement centers carry "gingerbread" trim and other typically Victorian types of trim, which can

be cut and installed pretty painlessly. Likewise, prefabricated shutters and window boxes in period styles are also easy to locate and install. To continue the theme, scout around antique stores for stained glass panels or windows, or buy reproduction stained glass pieces, and replace ready-made shed windows with them (do a lot of measuring to make sure they will fit!). Top the shed off with a classic Victorian weather vane, cupola, or both (some home improvement centers and *lots* of mail order companies sell these), and paint the shed and trim in pretty, contrasting colors!

## NAUTICAL CABANA

**P**ool areas are places for relaxation and recreation—fun. Whether you use a prefab building as a storage-only space for pool equipment and accessories, or as a small changing-room or cabana, it's fun to dress it up a bit. By painting a small cabana in bright colors that match your poolside decorating palette and adding a stencilled and painted border of waves (sea horses, fish, or whatever else your imagination conjures), you can achieve a fresh, playful look. Attaching pretty striped awnings both livens up an otherwise ordinary structure, at the same time providing shaded spots to which you can pull up a chair and cool off. Top off the cabana with a mermaid, fish, or ship weather vane to carry through the nautical theme! We've shown an octagonal structure, which can be purchased through some companies specializing in utility buildings— but the same design idea can easily be applied to a more commonly found square or rectangular building.

# SANTA FE SHED

Whether or not you actually live among the cacti and coyotes, decorative painting techniques such as the one shown on this simple shed can give a ready-made or old shed a finish that manages to be at once rustic and polished. The technique illustrated, of layering different colors of paint and sanding back into them, is referred to as "distressing," and creates a soft, weathered look, as if the walls have been slowly, gently worn by sun and wind over years. We've shown the technique used with natural hues, but almost any combination of colors can work together in order to best complement your landscape. If the "distressed" finish isn't quite what you're after but you're interested in trying out a new technique, pick up a good book on decorative painting (there are several) and check out the options: stippling, spattering, rag rolling, and combing (if you want to get outrageous, even marbling!) techniques could all achieve interesting effects used singly or in careful combination on a shed.

## COLORIST HIDEAWAY

The fastest, easiest way to liven up a ready-made shed is to simply paint it, and even a coat or two of one nice color that matches or complements your house and other buildings on the property can make a big difference in a kit-shed's contribution to your landscape. Why stop at a single hue, though? You may not want to go psychedelic, but by choosing a hand-ful of colors that work well together and alternat-ing them on the walls, door(s), and trim, you can achieve an effect that is sophisticated or perky, subtle or outrageous. If your own favorite colors don't make for an optimal combination, develop a palette by looking at uses of color by favorite painters or other artists.

# CIRCUS WAGON PLAYHOUSE

It's not easy to locate a child who doesn't want a place of his or her own to play, and while happenstance "forts" under the dining room table can sometimes do the trick, there's nothing quite like a real playhouse. There are probably as many ideas for transforming a dull structure into a fabulous, imaginative playhouse as there are kids. But, after all, you may not want, say, a neon-orange structure with chartreuse smiley faces and purple unicorns in the yard ... Here's an idea that provides an unusual, appealing retreat for small children while not proving an eyesore for you. Start by choosing a structure that's safe for children, finish it in bright opaque colors, then stencil clowns, circus animals, and other cheerful motifs on the outside walls. (Or cover the walls with your child's favorite storybook characters; both toy and craft stores are good supply stops for kid-friendly stencils.) Make or buy a festive flag and fly it from the rooftop, then find some old wagon wheels at a secondhand store or salvage yard, and partially bury them at the shed's four corners, and voilà! A jolly place for play sure to put smiles on little faces.

## RECYCLED "TIN-CAN" SHED

**O**ffbeat looks such as this one aren't everyone's cup of tea, but if you have a shed tucked away in the back yard and your tastes run to funky, it can be simple and fun to effect this transformation. We've gone whole hog, with sconces and window boxes made of old coffee cans and other recycled metal containers. (Using a drill to bore holes in these will allow you to easily screw or nail them to wood surfaces; you may need a circular saw with a metal-cutting blade to cut the cans to desired shapes.) Along with creating a unique and playful appearance for your shed, this decorating mode offers an extra bonus for flea market and

antique store junkies. In addition to putting aside interesting cans used in your own household to embellish the shed, you can keep an eye out for exotic or eye-catching containers, and amass a collection that will allow you to use cans and/or their lids or bottoms in patterns. (It might be fun to get friends and neighbors in on the act, and have them contribute interesting metal cans and other bits and pieces to the project.) Old metal drums once used to contain oil or other substances, rescued from s salvage yard and arranged in the landscape surrounding the shed and planted with bright blooms and trailing greenery, can add a great touch.

# CHAPTER EIGHT

# INSPIRATION

**W**hether big or small, simple or elaborate, garden sheds and structures, like other types of buildings, can have different "personalities." As you plan your shed, you'll find out what kind of shed best suits your personality and needs. For fun, here's a sprinkling of sheds and other backyard buildings that range from ordinary to extraordinary, to show a range of design possibilities and give you food for thought.

*Owner Charlie Walton designed this intriguing garden shed and gave it to his wife April to celebrate their wedding anniversary. Each face of the structure has a symbol cut out and backed with colored glass, with each symbol offering a special meaning: moon for woman, sun for man, heart for love, and a pine tree because their anniversary is in December.*

*Right: This potting shed of post-and-beam construction was designed and built by owners Pat and Debra Hudson, reusing materials from an old carriage shed.*

*Below: The covered, paved porch on this garden shed offers an inviting place for potting and other gardening work, even in rainy weather.*

*Below: This large garden shed just outside Greenville, South Carolina, is used mainly for keeping gardening tools, equipment, and paraphernalia safe and dry. But a small covered porch in the front also provides a place for morning coffee and afternoon tea for the Kings, its owners.*

*Right: Modeled after a 15th-century English "lych-gate" ( a roofed structure in churchyard providing shelter during burial services), this interesting Tudor-style structure enhances the English Garden at Stan Hywet Hall and Gardens in Akron, Ohio.*

*Two pretty Scandinavian sheds: left: rustic shed with sod roof tucked away on a Norwegian back-road; right: quaint octagonal summer-house on a Swedish riverbank.*

*William Cahill used water reed, wheat straw, steel hooks and lengths, and hazel wood scallops to thatch (in English/Irish style) the roof for this romantic garden shed in Indiana.*

*This charming garden shed, thatched by William Cahill in a combination of Irish, English, and other European styles, includes an unusual feature—the small, outcropping structure on the right is a hutch for pet rabbits.*

Overlooking Lake Pepin in Wisconsin, architect James Stageberg's estate "Wind Whistle" includes myriad garden houses, sheds, and other structures of his own design. *Top left: Functional and fun, this beautiful, rainbow-hued garden house includes a shed in the back and a screened porch for whiling away the hours. Bottom left: This unique garden overlook is a treasured spot for relaxing and watching the garden's progress.*

*Top and bottom right: At the same time elegant and whimsical, these two small backyard buildings provide separate space for work and relaxation.*

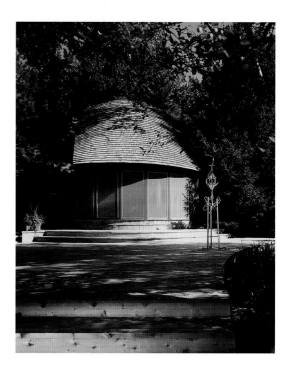

Though the seeming locations of this upside down shed's roof, doors, windows, and other parts make it look wholly dysfunctional, it actually makes a wonderful potting shed for owners John and Kathleen Holmes, who constructed it from recycled materials.

Turning sheds into art: top: At artist Bob Comings' Nada Farm Museum of Archetypes (NFMOA) in California, the "Gardenshed" is one of several buildings on the grounds toured by visitors. Built of recycled redwood and originally used as a chicken coop, the shed now houses gardening tools and supplies. Since 1978, Comings has added an evolving collection of objects, images, and decorations to its wall surfaces. The walls also function as places to "store" found objects used in Comings' art work; the south wall, for example, which gets the most rain and sun, plays host to objects made of rust and wood which, once weathered, may find a place in one of the pieces he creates. Bottom: As a soldier during World War II, Hungarian cobbler Jozsef Balogh admired a fantastically decorated house in Poland, and vowed to one day create one of his own. Today, in the village of Pribenik, Hungary, where he lives, Balogh's marvelous shed is a folk tradition all its own. Covered with an inventive mosaic of doctored pop bottles, tiny colored rocks, cloth, newspapers and other text, caps, dolls, and just about anything else you can name, it also boasts a rooftop clock that comes in handy to passersby.

PLANS (AND ADDITIONAL MATERIALS AND TOOLS LISTS)
NOTE: ALL PLANS SHOULD BE ENLARGED TO SCALE.

## THE SHED-ROOFED POTTING SHED

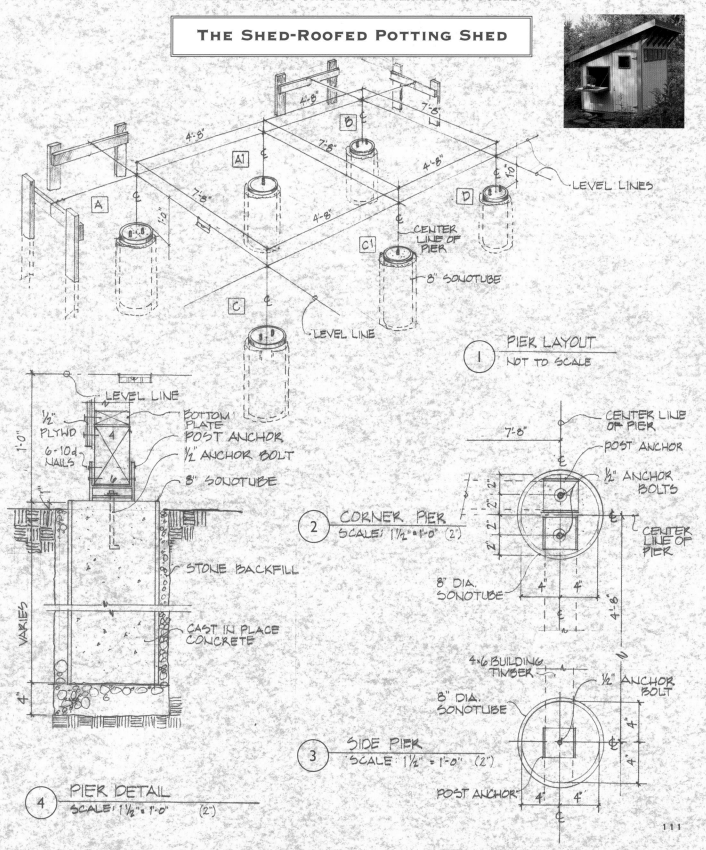

LEVEL LINES

4'-8"

7'-8"

4'-8"

1'-0"

CENTER LINE OF PIER

8" SONOTUBE

LEVEL LINE

① PIER LAYOUT
NOT TO SCALE

LEVEL LINE

½" PLYWD

4

BOTTOM PLATE
POST ANCHOR
½" ANCHOR BOLT

6-10d NAILS

8" SONOTUBE

1'-0"

STONE BACKFILL

VARIES

CAST IN PLACE CONCRETE

4"

④ PIER DETAIL
SCALE: 1½" = 1'-0"    (2")

CENTER LINE OF PIER

7'-8"

POST ANCHOR

½" ANCHOR BOLTS

CENTER LINE OF PIER

② CORNER PIER
SCALE: 1½" = 1'-0"  (2")

8" DIA. SONOTUBE

4"    4"

4'-8"

4x6 BUILDING TIMBER

8" DIA. SONOTUBE

½" ANCHOR BOLT

4"

4"

③ SIDE PIER
SCALE: 1½" = 1'-0"  (2")

POST ANCHOR

4"    4"

# THE SHED-ROOFED POTTING SHED

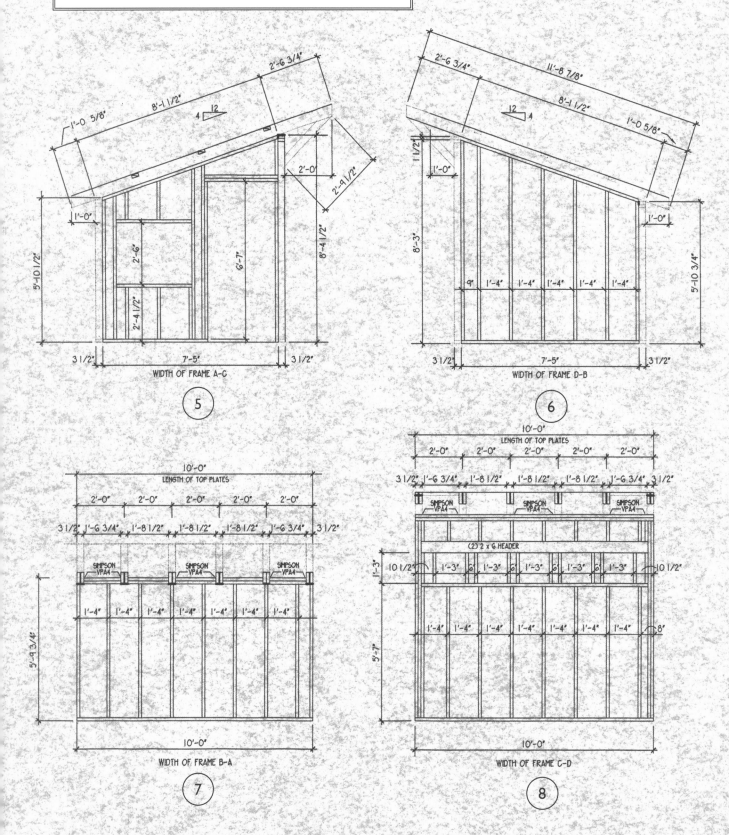

**5**

WIDTH OF FRAME A-C

2'-6 3/4"
8'-1 1/2"
4 | 12
1'-0 5/8"
1'-0"
5'-10 1/2"
2'-6"
6'-7"
2'-4 1/2"
2'-0'
2'-9 1/2"
8'-4 1/2"
3 1/2"
7'-5"
3 1/2"

**6**

WIDTH OF FRAME D-B

2'-6 3/4"
11'-8 7/8"
12 | 4
8'-1 1/2"
1'-0 5/8"
1 1/2"
1'-0"
1'-0"
8'-3"
5'-10 3/4"
9"  1'-4"  1'-4"  1'-4"  1'-4"  1'-4"
3 1/2"
7'-5"
3 1/2"

**7**

WIDTH OF FRAME B-A

10'-0"
LENGTH OF TOP PLATES
2'-0"  2'-0"  2'-0"  2'-0"  2'-0"
3 1/2" 1'-6 3/4" 1'-8 1/2" 1'-8 1/2" 1'-8 1/2" 1'-6 3/4" 3 1/2"
SIMPSON VPA4   SIMPSON VPA4   SIMPSON VPA4
1'-4" 1'-4" 1'-4" 1'-4" 1'-4" 1'-4" 1'-4"
5'-9 3/4"
10'-0"

**8**

WIDTH OF FRAME C-D

10'-0"
LENGTH OF TOP PLATES
2'-0"  2'-0"  2'-0"  2'-0"  2'-0"
3 1/2" 1'-6 3/4" 1'-8 1/2" 1'-8 1/2" 1'-8 1/2" 1'-6 3/4" 3 1/2"
SIMPSON VPA4   SIMPSON VPA4   SIMPSON VPA4
(2) 2 x 6 HEADER
1'-3"
10 1/2"  1'-3" 6 1'-3" 6 1'-3" 6 1'-3" 6 1'-3"  10 1/2"
5'-7"
1'-4" 1'-4" 1'-4" 1'-4" 1'-4" 1'-4" 1'-4"  8"
10'-0"

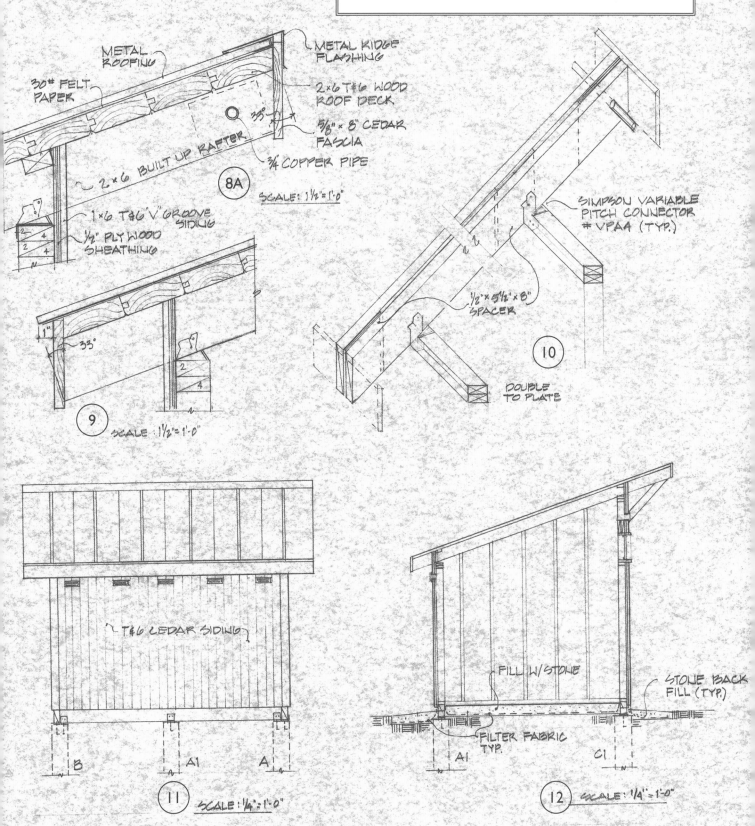

METAL RIDGE FLASHING

METAL ROOFING

30# FELT PAPER

2×6 T&G WOOD ROOF DECK

⅝" × 8" CEDAR FASCIA

¾ COPPER PIPE

35°

2×6 BUILT UP RAFTER

**8A** SCALE: 1½"=1'-0"

1×6 T&G "V" GROOVE SIDING

½" PLYWOOD SHEATHING

2  4
2  4

1"

35°

6

2
4

**9** SCALE: 1½"=1'-0"

SIMPSON VARIABLE PITCH CONNECTOR # VPA4 (TYP.)

½" × 5½" × 8" SPACER

**10**

DOUBLE TO PLATE

T&G CEDAR SIDING

B        A1        A

**11** SCALE: ¼"=1'-0"

FILL W/ STONE

STONE BACK FILL (TYP.)

FILTER FABRIC TYP.

A1        C1

**12** SCALE: ¼"=1'-0"

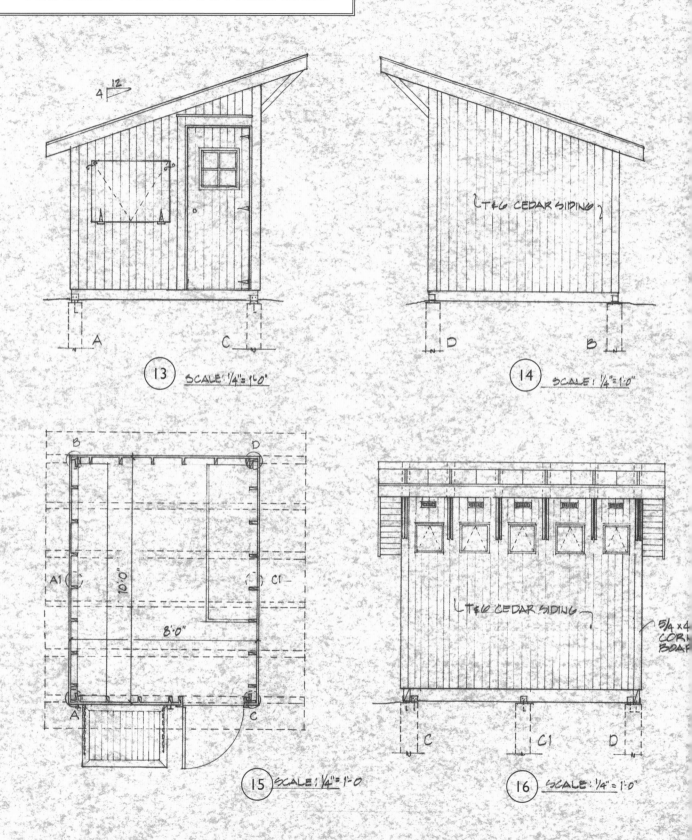

4 $\frac{12}{}$

A          C

**13**    SCALE: 1/4"= 1'-0"

T&G CEDAR SIDING

D          B

**14**    SCALE: 1/4"= 1'-0"

B          D

A1          C1

10'-0"

8'-0"

A          C

**15**    SCALE: 1/4"= 1'-0"

T&G CEDAR SIDING

5/4 x 4
CORN
BOAR

C          C1          D

**16**    SCALE: 1/4"= 1'-0"

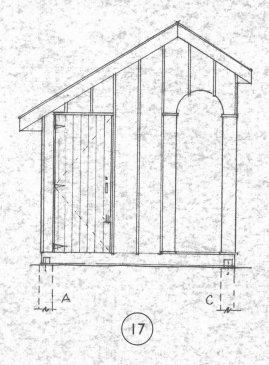

(17)

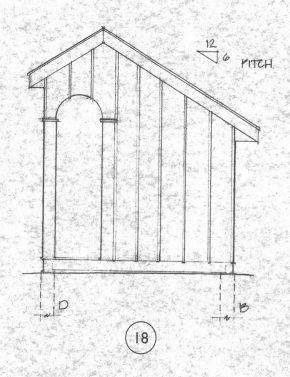

12
6  PITCH.

(18)

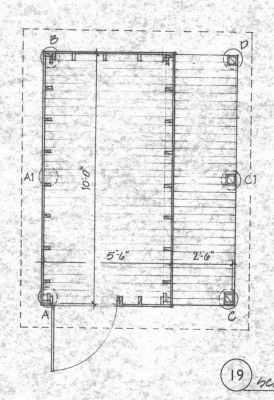

B

10'-0"

5'-6"    2'-6"

A1

C1

A

C

(19) SCALE: 1/4" = 1'-0"

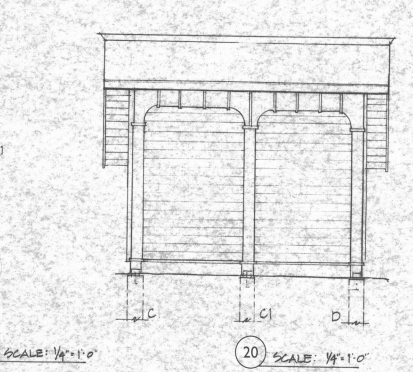

C    C1    D

(20) SCALE: 1/4" = 1'-0"

## DUAL-USE STORAGE SHED (SH-2)

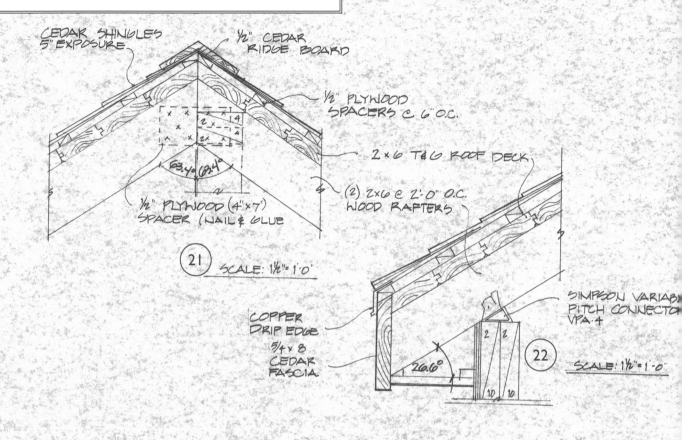

CEDAR SHINGLES
5" EXPOSURE

½" CEDAR
RIDGE BOARD

½" PLYWOOD
SPACERS @ 6" O.C.

2 × 6 T&G ROOF DECK

(2) 2×6 @ 2'-0" O.C.
WOOD RAFTERS

63.4° (63.4°)

½" PLYWOOD (4"×7")
SPACER (NAIL & GLUE

21   SCALE: 1½"=1'-0"

COPPER
DRIP EDGE

5/4 × 8
CEDAR
FASCIA

SIMPSON VARIABLE
PITCH CONNECTOR
VPA-4

26.6°

22   SCALE: 1½"=1'-0"

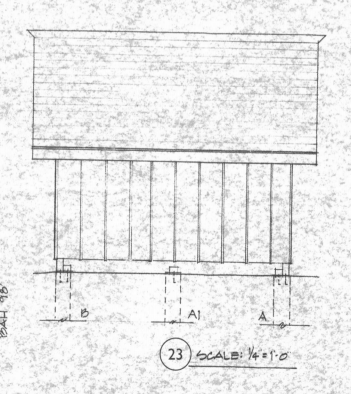

B          A1          A

23   SCALE: ¼"=1'-0"

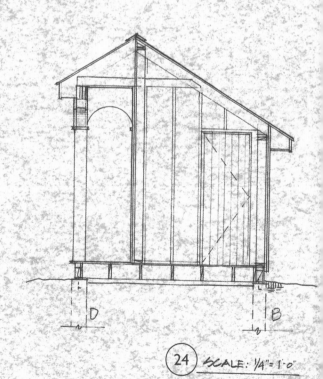

D                    B

24   SCALE: ¼"=1'-0"

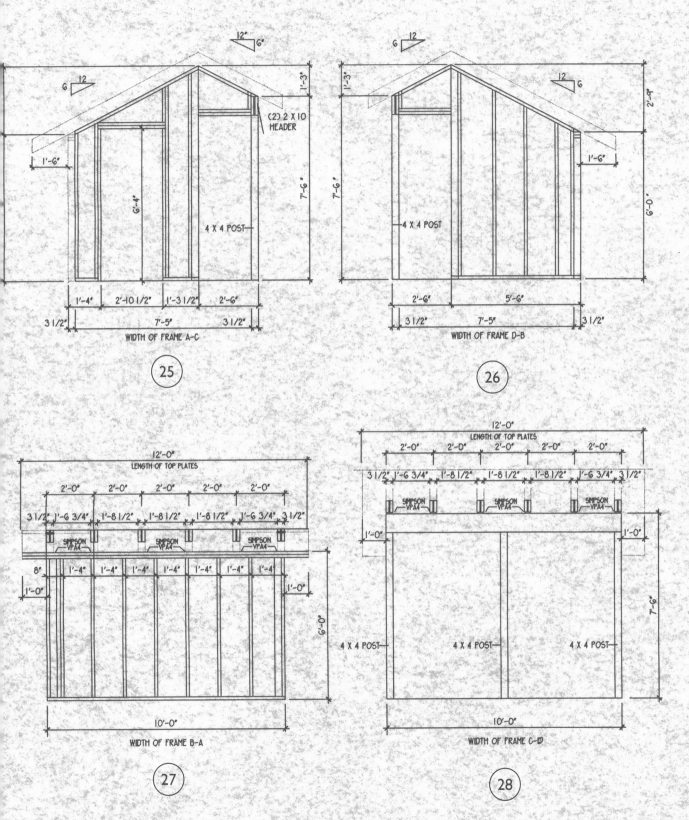

12" / 6"

6 / 12

(2) 2 X 10 HEADER

1'-3"

1'-6"

6'-4"

4 X 4 POST

7'-6"

1'-4"  2'-10 1/2"  1'-3 1/2"  2'-6"

3 1/2"  7'-5"  3 1/2"

WIDTH OF FRAME A-C

25

6 / 12

12 / 6

1'-3"

2'-4"

4 X 4 POST

1'-6"

6'-0"

7'-6"

2'-6"  5'-6"

3 1/2"  7'-5"  3 1/2"

WIDTH OF FRAME D-B

26

12'-0"
LENGTH OF TOP PLATES

2'-0"  2'-0"  2'-0"  2'-0"  2'-0"

3 1/2"  1'-6 3/4"  1'-8 1/2"  1'-8 1/2"  1'-8 1/2"  1'-6 3/4"  3 1/2"

SIMPSON VPA4    SIMPSON VPA4    SIMPSON VPA4

8"  1'-4"  1'-4"  1'-4"  1'-4"  1'-4"  1'-4"  1'-4"

1'-0"  1'-0"

6'-0"

10'-0"

WIDTH OF FRAME B-A

27

12'-0"
LENGTH OF TOP PLATES

2'-0"  2'-0"  2'-0"  2'-0"  2'-0"

3 1/2"  1'-6 3/4"  1'-8 1/2"  1'-8 1/2"  1'-8 1/2"  1'-6 3/4"  3 1/2"

SIMPSON VPA4    SIMPSON VPA4    SIMPSON VPA4

1'-0"  1'-0"

7'-6"

4 X 4 POST    4 X 4 POST    4 X 4 POST

10'-0"

WIDTH OF FRAME C-D

28

# DUAL-USE STORAGE SHED (SH-2)

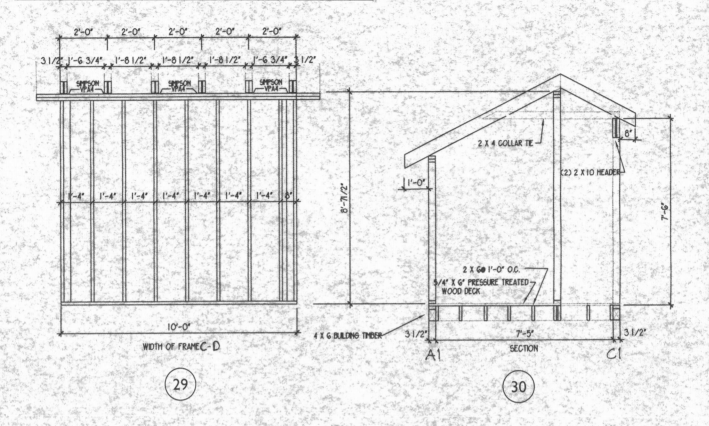

WIDTH OF FRAME C-D

29

SECTION

30

## ADDITIONAL TOOLS

### POWER MITER BOX

**Table Saw** (*Note*: For this and other variations in this section, a table saw is required for cutting cedar strips for the battens for board and batten siding. If you would rather bypass the table saw, a local lumberyard can make the cuts for you.)

## ADDITIONAL MATERIALS AND SUPPLIES

| DESCRIPTION | QTY. | MATERIAL | DIMENSIONS |
|---|---|---|---|
| roofing | 2 sq. | standard–width | |
| cedar shingles | 16" long | | |
| roofing | 2 | copper drip | 12' long |
| ridge cap | 2 | cedar 1 x 6s | 12' long |
| siding | 15 | cedar 1 x 12s | 12' long |
| siding | 20 | 1½" x ¾" cedar battens | 10' long |
| siding | 24 | cedar clapboards | 5½" x 10' |
| door | 1 | ½" CDX plywood | 4' x 8' |
| door | 6 | tongue-and-groove cedar | 6" x 8' |

# FRENCH PAVILION (SH-3)

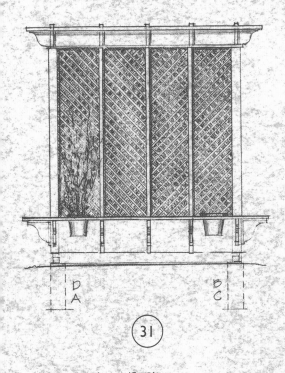

(31)

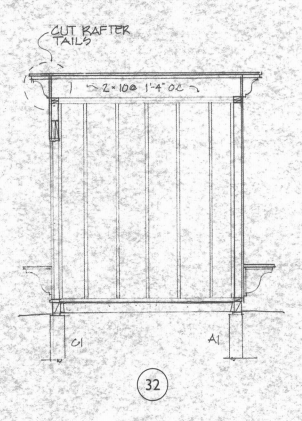

CUT RAFTER TAILS

~2×10 @ 1'-4" OC~

C1    A1

(32)

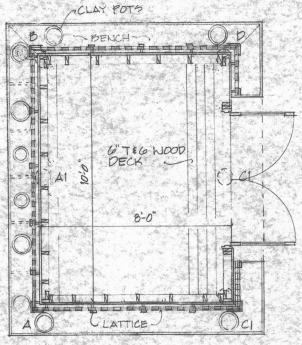

CLAY POTS

BENCH

B          D

6" T&G WOOD DECK

A1    10'-0"

8'-0"

C1

A          C1

LATTICE

(33)  SCALE: 1/4"=1'-0"

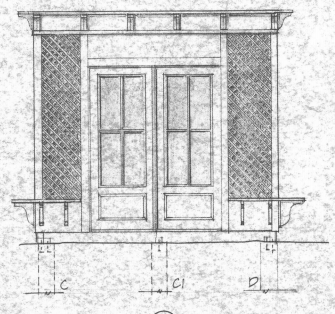

C      C1      D

(34)  SCALE: 1/4"=1'-0"

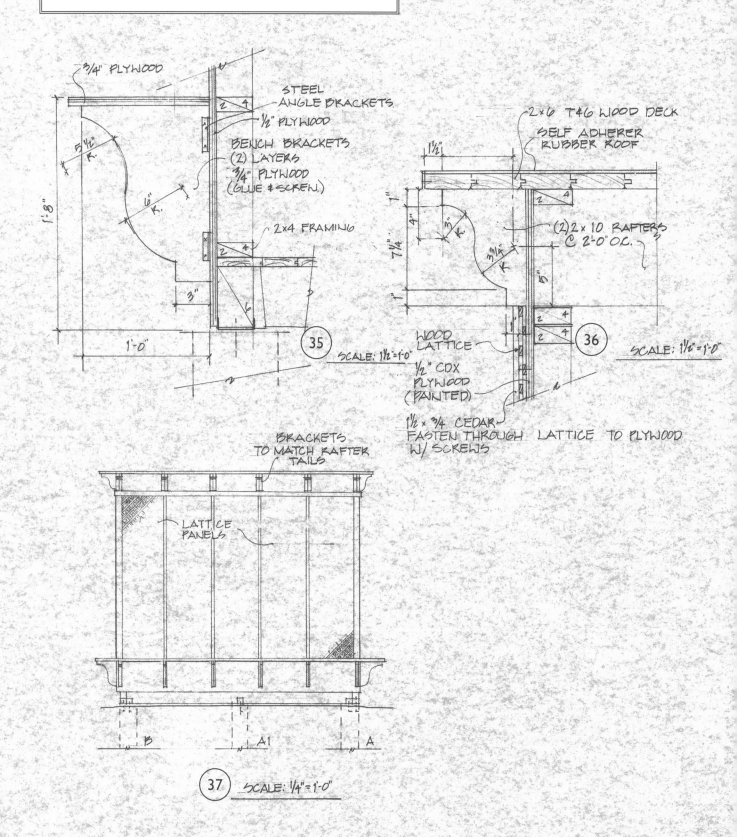

3/4" PLYWOOD

STEEL ANGLE BRACKETS

1/2" PLYWOOD

BENCH BRACKETS (2) LAYERS 3/4" PLYWOOD (GLUE & SCREW)

2×4 FRAMING

5 1/2" R.

6" R.

1'-8"

3"

1'-0"

35    SCALE: 1 1/2"=1'-0"

2×6 T&G WOOD DECK

SELF ADHERER RUBBER ROOF

1 1/2"

1"

4"

3"

3 3/4" R.

R.

(2) 2×10 RAFTERS @ 2'-0" O.C.

7 1/4"

5"

1"

WOOD LATTICE

1/2" CDX PLYWOOD (PAINTED)

36    SCALE: 1 1/2"=1'-0"

1 1/2 × 3/4 CEDAR FASTEN THROUGH LATTICE TO PLYWOOD W/ SCREWS

BRACKETS TO MATCH RAFTER TAILS

LATTICE PANELS

B    A1    A

37    SCALE: 1/4"=1'-0"

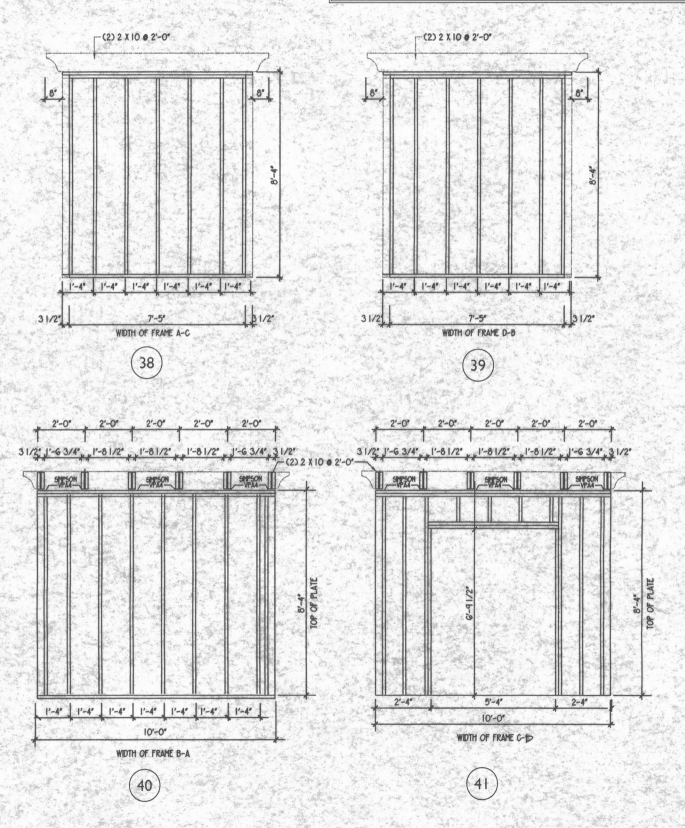

(2) 2 X 10 @ 2'-0"

8"                    8"

8'-4"

1'-4" | 1'-4" | 1'-4" | 1'-4" | 1'-4" | 1'-4"

3 1/2"        7'-5"        3 1/2"

WIDTH OF FRAME A-C

38

(2) 2 X 10 @ 2'-0"

8"                    8"

8'-4"

1'-4" | 1'-4" | 1'-4" | 1'-4" | 1'-4" | 1'-4"

3 1/2"        7'-5"        3 1/2"

WIDTH OF FRAME D-B

39

2'-0"   2'-0"   2'-0"   2'-0"   2'-0"

3 1/2" 1'-6 3/4" 1'-8 1/2" 1'-8 1/2" 1'-8 1/2" 1'-6 3/4" 3 1/2"

(2) 2 X 10 @ 2'-0"

SIMPSON VPA4    SIMPSON VPA4    SIMPSON VPA4

8'-4"

TOP OF PLATE

1'-4" | 1'-4" | 1'-4" | 1'-4" | 1'-4" | 1'-4" | 1'-4"

10'-0"

WIDTH OF FRAME B-A

40

2'-0"   2'-0"   2'-0"   2'-0"   2'-0"

3 1/2" 1'-6 3/4" 1'-8 1/2" 1'-8 1/2" 1'-8 1/2" 1'-6 3/4" 3 1/2"

SIMPSON VPA4    SIMPSON VPA4    SIMPSON VPA4

6'-9 1/2"

8'-4"

TOP OF PLATE

2'-4"       5'-4"       2-4"

10'-0"

WIDTH OF FRAME C-D

41

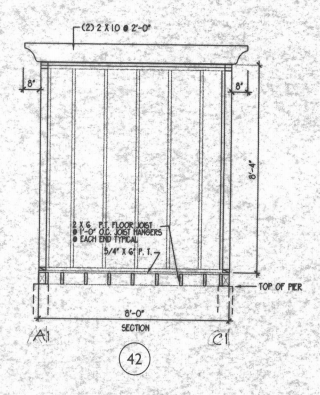

- (2) 2 X 10 @ 2'-0"

8'

8'

8'-4"

2 X 6 P.T. FLOOR JOIST
@ 1'-0" O.C. JOIST HANGERS
@ EACH END TYPICAL

5/4" X 6' P.T.

TOP OF PIER

8'-0"

SECTION

A1    C1

42

## ADDITIONAL TOOLS REQUIRED

Power Miter Box

## ADDITIONAL MATERIALS AND SUPPLIES REQUIRED

| DESCRIPTION | QTY. | MATERIAL | DIMENSIONS |
|---|---|---|---|
| Roofing | 1 roll | self-adhering rubber roofing | 4' x 34' |
|  | 2 | copper drip | 10' long |
|  | 2 | copper drip | 12' long |
| Siding | 9 | prefabricated lattice | 4' x 8' |
|  | 10 | 1½" x ¾" cedar battens | 8' long |
|  | 18 | pine furring 1 x 2s | 8' long |
| Corners | 1 | cedar 1 x 4s | 8' long |
| Doors | 2 | custom/salvaged French doors | 5' 3½" x 6' 9¼" |
| Potting Bench | 3 | ¾" CDX plywood | 4' x 8' |

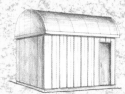

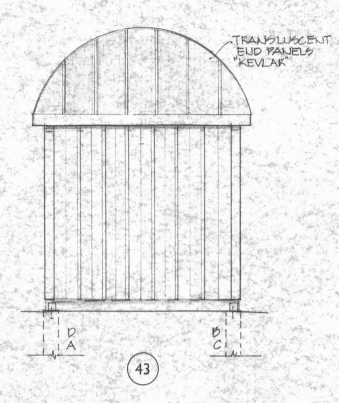

TRANSLUSCENT
END PANELS
"KEVLAR"

(43)

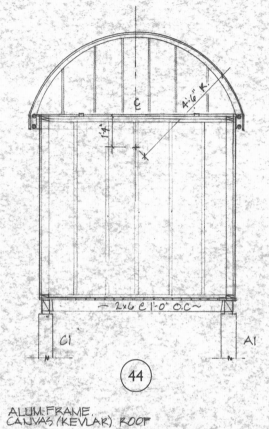

14"

4'-6" K.

~ 2x6 C 1'-0" O.C ~

C1                    A1

(44)

CANOPY ROOF ABOVE

B                                    D

10'-0"

T&G WOOD
DECK

A1                                    C1

8'-0"

ROOF
LINE

A                                    C

(45)    SCALE: 1/4"=1'-0"

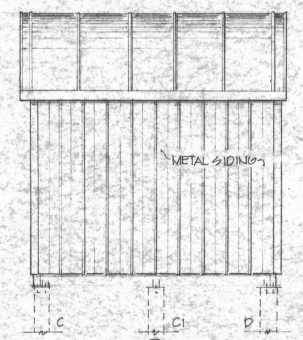

ALUM. FRAME.
CANVAS (KEVLAR) ROOF

METAL SIDING

C          C1          D

(46)    SCALE: 1/4"=1'-0"

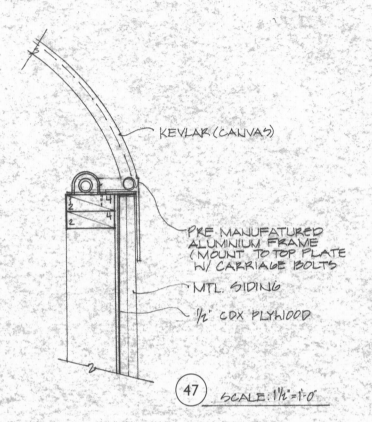

KEVLAR (CANVAS)

PRE-MANUFATURED
ALUMINIUM FRAME
( MOUNT TO TOP PLATE
W/ CARRIAGE BOLTS

MTL. SIDING

½" CDX PLYWOOD

47  SCALE: 1½"=1'-0"

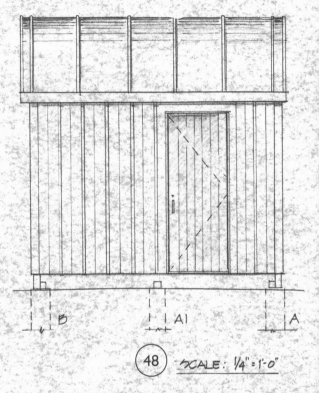

B          A1          A

48  SCALE: ¼"=1'-0"

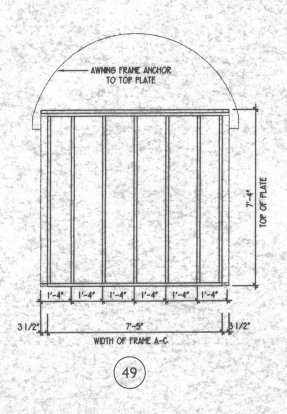

AWNING FRAME ANCHOR
TO TOP PLATE

TOP OF PLATE
7'-4"

1'-4" 1'-4" 1'-4" 1'-4" 1'-4" 1'-4"

3 1/2"    7'-5"    3 1/2"

WIDTH OF FRAME A-C

49

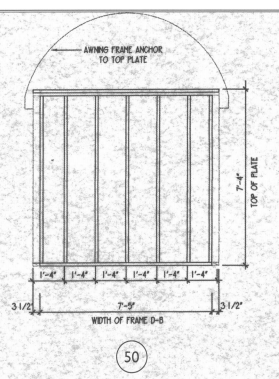

AWNING FRAME ANCHOR
TO TOP PLATE

TOP OF PLATE
7'-4"

1'-4" 1'-4" 1'-4" 1'-4" 1'-4" 1'-4"

3 1/2"    7'-5"    3 1/2"

WIDTH OF FRAME D-B

50

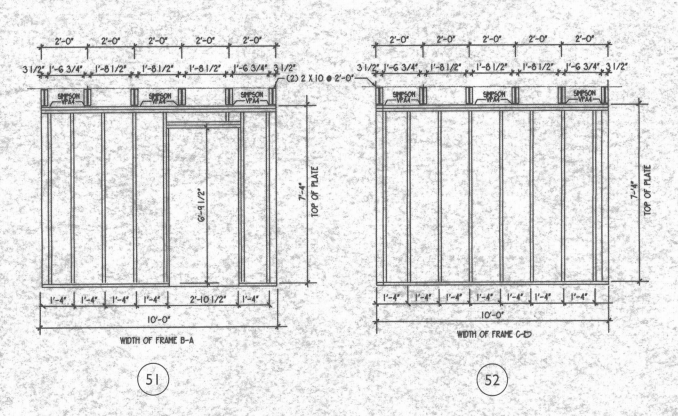

2'-0"  2'-0"  2'-0"  2'-0"  2'-0"

3 1/2" 1'-6 3/4" 1'-8 1/2" 1'-8 1/2" 1'-8 1/2" 1'-6 3/4" 3 1/2"

(2) 2 X 10 @ 2'-0"

SIMPSON VPA4   SIMPSON VPA4   SIMPSON VPA4

TOP OF PLATE
7'-4"

6'-9 1/2"

1'-4" 1'-4" 1'-4" 1'-4" 2'-10 1/2" 1'-4"

10'-0"

WIDTH OF FRAME B-A

51

2'-0"  2'-0"  2'-0"  2'-0"  2'-0"

3 1/2" 1'-6 3/4" 1'-8 1/2" 1'-8 1/2" 1'-8 1/2" 1'-6 3/4" 3 1/2"

SIMPSON VPA4   SIMPSON VPA4   SIMPSON VPA4

TOP OF PLATE
7'-4"

1'-4" 1'-4" 1'-4" 1'-4" 1'-4" 1'-4" 1'-4"

10'-0"

WIDTH OF FRAME C-D

52

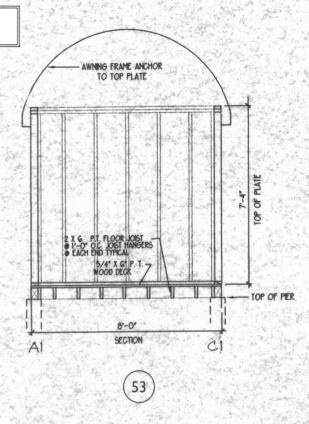

AWNING FRAME ANCHOR
TO TOP PLATE

7'-4"   TOP OF PLATE

2 X 6  P.T. FLOOR JOIST
1'-0" O.C. JOIST HANGERS
EACH END TYPICAL

5/4" X 6" P.T.
WOOD DECK

TOP OF PIER

8'-0"

SECTION

A1          C1

53

## ADDITIONAL TOOLS REQUIRED

Wrench or Ratchet Wrench

## ADDITIONAL MATERIALS AND SUPPLIES

| DESCRIPTION | QTY. | MATERIAL | DIMENSIONS |
|---|---|---|---|
| Roofing | 1 | pre-manufactured aluminum | 9' x 11' |
| frame with canvas roof, | | | |
| translucent end (6" overhang) | | | |
| panels and manufacturer's fasteners | | | |
| Siding | 160 sq. ft. | pre-finished metal siding | (order to length) |
| Corners for metal siding | 4 | pre-manufactured corners | 7' 4" long |
| Door | 1 | ½" CDX plywood | 4' x 8' |
| | 6 | tongue-and groove cedar | 6" x 8' |

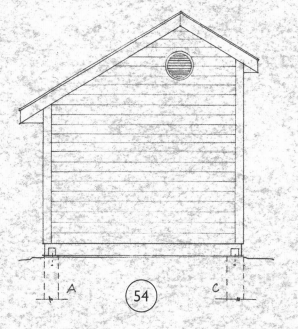

54

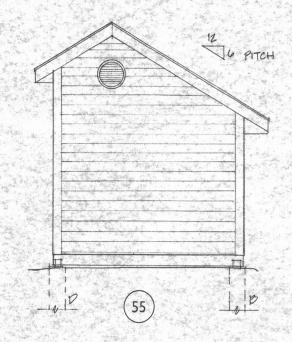

12
6 PITCH

55

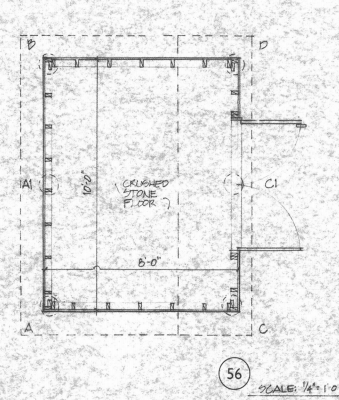

B                    D

A1

10'-0"

CRUSHED
STONE
FLOOR

C1

8'-0"

A                    C

56    SCALE: 1/4"= 1'-0"

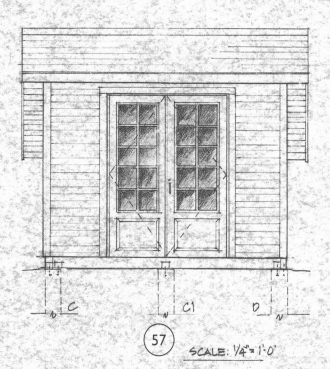

C        C1        D

57    SCALE: 1/4"= 1'-0"

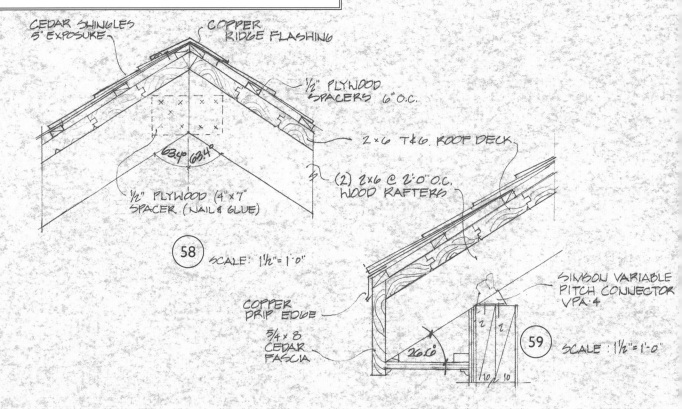

CEDAR SHINGLES 5" EXPOSURE

COPPER RIDGE FLASHING

1/2" PLYWOOD SPACERS 6" O.C.

2×6 T&G ROOF DECK

(2) 2×6 @ 2'-0" O.C. WOOD RAFTERS

63.4° 63.4°

1/2" PLYWOOD (4"×7") SPACER (NAIL & GLUE)

(58) SCALE: 1 1/2" = 1'-0"

COPPER DRIP EDGE

5/4 × 8 CEDAR FASCIA

26.6°

SIMPSON VARIABLE PITCH CONNECTOR VPA-4

2  2

10  10

(59) SCALE: 1 1/2" = 1'-0"

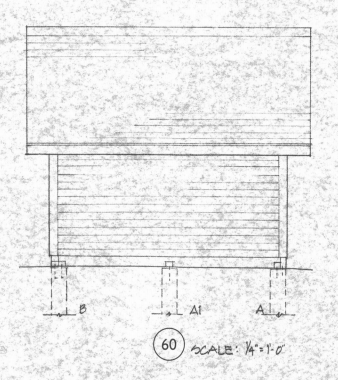

B    A1    A

(60) SCALE: 1/4" = 1'-0"

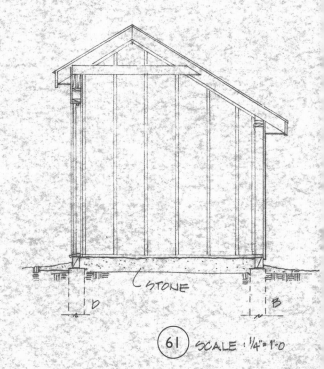

STONE

D    B

(61) SCALE: 1/4" = 1'-0"

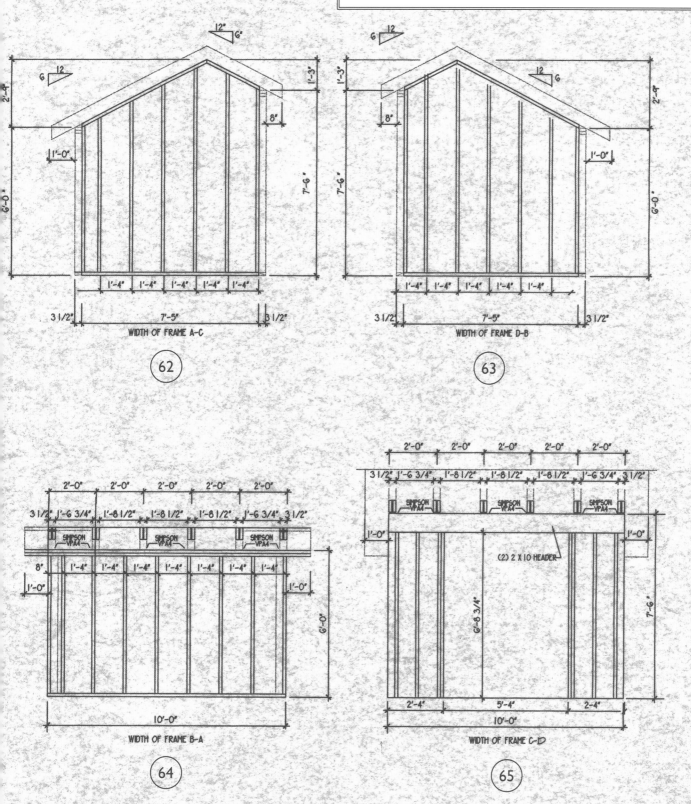

12" ⊿ 6"

6 ⊿ 12

6 ⊿ 12

2'-4"

1'-3"

8"

1'-0"

6'-0"

7'-6"

1'-4" 1'-4" 1'-4" 1'-4" 1'-4"

3 1/2"

7'-5"

3 1/2"

WIDTH OF FRAME A-C

62

6 ⊿ 12

1'-3"

2'-4"

8"

7'-6"

1'-0"

6'-0"

1'-4" 1'-4" 1'-4" 1'-4" 1'-4"

3 1/2"

7'-5"

3 1/2"

WIDTH OF FRAME D-B

63

2'-0" 2'-0" 2'-0" 2'-0" 2'-0"

3 1/2" 1'-6 3/4" 1'-8 1/2" 1'-8 1/2" 1'-8 1/2" 1'-6 3/4" 3 1/2"

SIMPSON VPA4  SIMPSON VPA4  SIMPSON VPA4

8"  1'-4" 1'-4" 1'-4" 1'-4" 1'-4" 1'-4" 1'-4"

1'-0"

1'-0"

6'-0"

10'-0"

WIDTH OF FRAME B-A

64

2'-0" 2'-0" 2'-0" 2'-0" 2'-0"

3 1/2" 1'-6 3/4" 1'-8 1/2" 1'-8 1/2" 1'-8 1/2" 1'-6 3/4" 3 1/2"

SIMPSON VPA4  SIMPSON VPA4  SIMPSON VPA4

1'-0"

1'-0"

(2) 2 X 10 HEADER

6'-6 3/4"

7'-6"

2'-4" 5'-4" 2'-4"

10'-0"

WIDTH OF FRAME C-D

65

# CLASSIC ALL-PURPOSE STORAGE SHED (SH-5)

## ADDITIONAL TOOLS REQUIRED

Power Miter Box

## ADDITIONAL MATERIALS AND SUPPLIES REQUIRED

| DESCRIPTION | QTY. | MATERIAL | DIMENSIONS |
|---|---|---|---|
| Roofing | 2 sq. | standard-width cedar shingles | 16" long |
| | 18 | pine furring 1 x 2s | 12' long |
| | 1 | copper ridge flashing | 12' long |
| siding | 20 | 1½" x ¾" cedar battens | 10' long |
| siding | 210 sq. ft. | cedar clapboards | 5½" x 10' |
| corners | 2 | cedar 1 x 4s | 12' long |
| door casing | 7 | cedar 1 x 4s | 8' long |
| doors | 2 | custom/salvaged French doors | 5' 3½" x 6' 8½" |
| ventilation louvre vent | 2 | pre-manufactured round | 1' diameter |

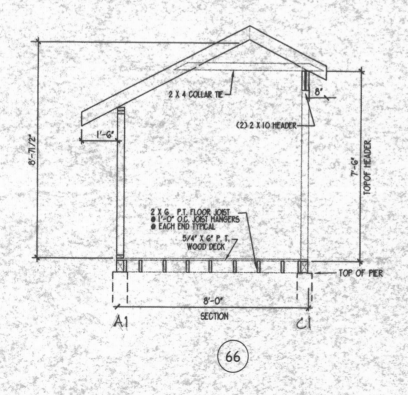

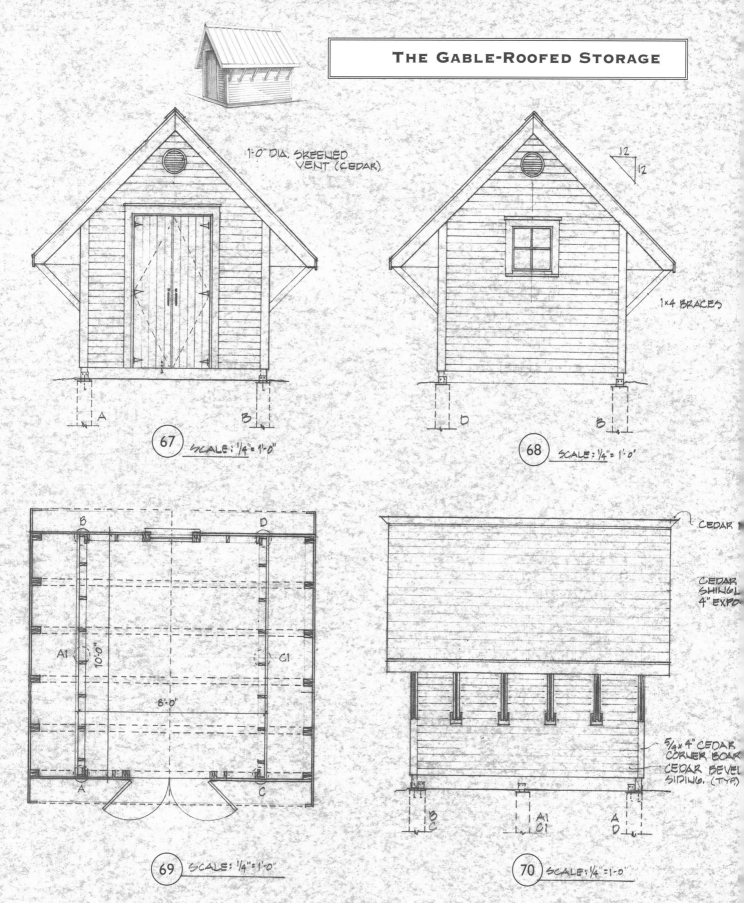

1'-0" DIA. SCREENED VENT (CEDAR)

A

B

67  SCALE: 1/4" = 1'-0"

12
12

1x4 BRACES

D

B

68  SCALE: 1/4" = 1'-0"

B                    D

A1                   C1

10'-0"

8'-0"

A                    C

69  SCALE: 1/4" = 1'-0"

CEDAR

CEDAR SHINGL 4" EXPO

5/4 x 4" CEDAR CORNER BOAR
CEDAR BEVEL SIDING (TYP)

B
C

A1
C1

A
D

70  SCALE: 1/4" = 1'-0"

# GABLED-ROOFED-STORAGE SHED

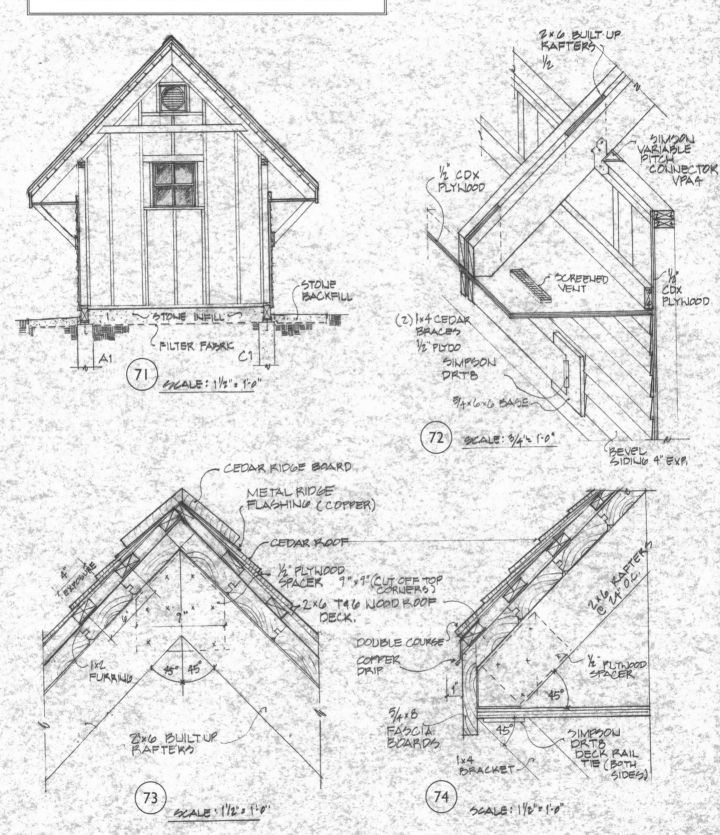

**71**  SCALE: 1½" = 1'-0"

STOVE BACKFILL

STONE INFILL

FILTER FABRIC

A1     C1

---

2×6 BUILT-UP RAFTERS

½

½" CDX PLYWOOD

SIMPSON VARIABLE PITCH CONNECTOR VPA4

½" CDX PLYWOOD

SCREENED VENT

(2) 1×4 CEDAR BRACES

½" PLYWD

SIMPSON DRT8

5/4×6×6 BASE

BEVEL SIDING 4" EXP.

**72**  SCALE: ¾" = 1'-0"

---

CEDAR RIDGE BOARD

METAL RIDGE FLASHING (COPPER)

CEDAR ROOF

½" PLYWOOD SPACER  9"×9" (CUT OFF TOP CORNERS)

2×6 T&6 WOOD ROOF DECK.

4" EXPOSURE

9"

45°  45°

1×2 FURRING

2×6 BUILT UP RAFTERS

**73**  SCALE: 1½" = 1'-0"

---

2×6 RAFTERS @ 24" O.C.

½" PLYWOOD SPACER

DOUBLE COURSE

COPPER DRIP

45°

1"

5/4×8 FASCIA BOARDS

45°

1×4 BRACKET

SIMPSON DRT8 DECK RAIL TIE (BOTH SIDES)

**74**  SCALE: 1½" = 1'-0"

# The Gable-Roofed Storage Shed

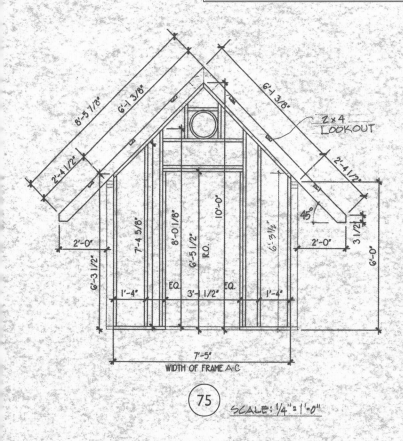

2 x 4
LOOKOUT

8'-5 1/8"  6'-1 3/8"  6'-1 3/8"

2'-4 1/2"  2'-4 1/2"

45°  3 1/2"

2'-0"  7'-4 5/8"  8'-01/8"  10'-0"  6'-3 1/2"  2'-0"  6'-0"

R.O.  6'-5 1/2"  R.O.

6'-3 1/2"

EQ.  EQ.

1'-4"  3'-1/2"  1'-4"

7'-5"

WIDTH OF FRAME A-C

(75)  SCALE: 1/4" = 1'-0"

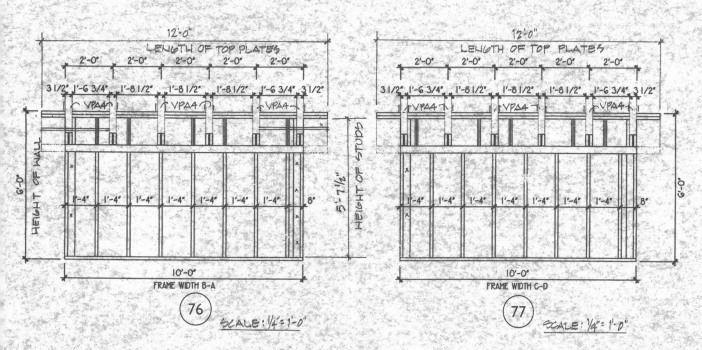

12'-0"
LENGTH OF TOP PLATES

2'-0"  2'-0"  2'-0"  2'-0"  2'-0"

3 1/2"  1'-6 3/4"  1'-8 1/2"  1'-8 1/2"  1'-8 1/2"  1'-6 3/4"  3 1/2"

VPA4  VPA4  VPA4

6'-0"  HEIGHT OF WALL

1'-4"  1'-4"  1'-4"  1'-4"  1'-4"  1'-4"  1'-4"  8"

10'-0"
FRAME WIDTH B-A

(76)  SCALE: 1/4" = 1'-0"

12'-0"
LENGTH OF TOP PLATES

2'-0"  2'-0"  2'-0"  2'-0"  2'-0"

3 1/2"  1'-6 3/4"  1'-8 1/2"  1'-8 1/2"  1'-8 1/2"  1'-6 3/4"  3 1/2"

VPA4  VPA4  VPA4

5'-7 1/2"  HEIGHT OF STUDS

6'-0"

1'-4"  1'-4"  1'-4"  1'-4"  1'-4"  1'-4"  1'-4"  8"

10'-0"
FRAME WIDTH C-D

(77)  SCALE: 1/4" = 1'-0"

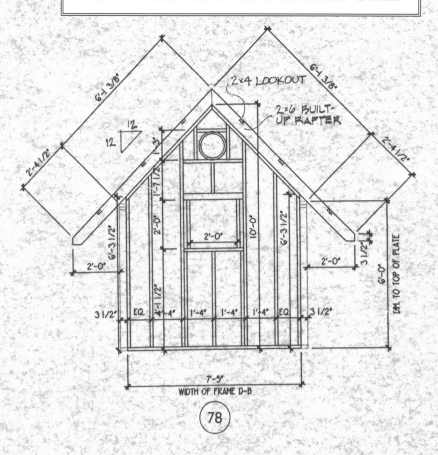

2×4 LOOKOUT

2×6 BUILT-UP RAFTER

6'-1 3/8"

6'-1 3/8"

2'-4 1/2"

2'-4 1/2"

12

12 12

1'-7 1/2"

6'-3 1/2"

6'-3 1/2"

2'-0"

10'-0"

2'-0"

2'-0"

2'-0"

3 1/2"

6'-0"

DIM. TO TOP OF PLATE

3 1/2" EQ 4'-4" 1'-4" 1'-4" 1'-4" EQ 3 1/2"

7'-5"

WIDTH OF FRAME D-B

(78)

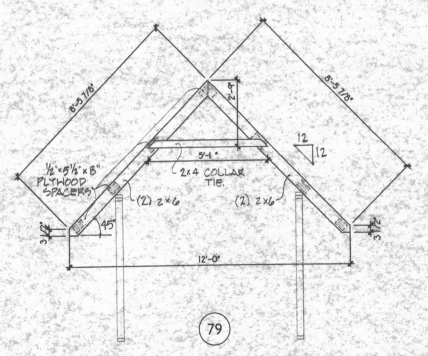

8'-5 7/8"

8'-5 7/8"

2'-0"

12 12

5'-1"

1/2" × 5 1/2" × 8" PLYWOOD SPACERS

2×4 COLLAR TIE.

(2) 2×6

(2) 2×6

3 1/2"

45

3 1/2"

12'-0"

(79)

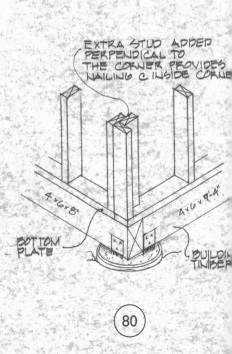

EXTRA STUD ADDED PERPENDICAL TO THE CORNER PROVIDES NAILING @ INSIDE CORNER

4×6×8"

4×6×9'-4"

BOTTOM PLATE

BUILDING TIMBER

(80)

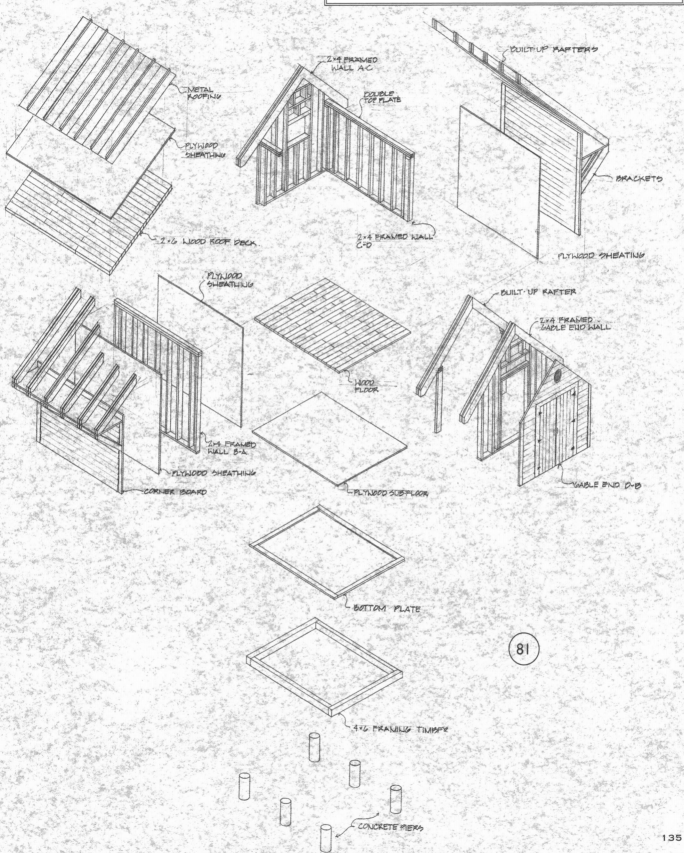

METAL ROOFING

PLYWOOD SHEATHING

2×6 WOOD ROOF DECK

2×4 FRAMED WALL A-C

DOUBLE TOP PLATE

2×4 FRAMED WALL C-D

BUILT-UP RAFTERS

BRACKETS

PLYWOOD SHEATING

PLYWOOD SHEATHING

2×4 FRAMED WALL B-A

PLYWOOD SHEATHING

CORNER BOARD

WOOD FLOOR

PLYWOOD SUBFLOOR

BUILT-UP RAFTER

2×4 FRAMED GABLE END WALL

GABLE END D-B

BOTTOM PLATE

81

4×6 FRAMING TIMBER

CONCRETE PIERS

135

# MINI-SHED WITH CANOPIED PORCH
## (GR-2)

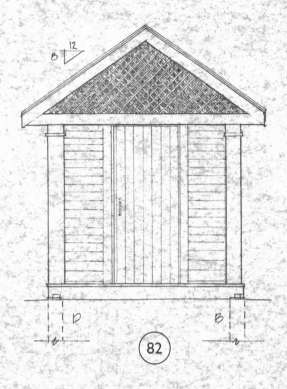

12
8

D          B

(82)

2×6 @ 1'-0"

A1          C1

(83)

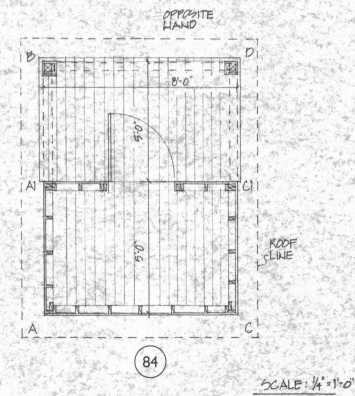

OPPOSITE
HAND

B          D

8'-0"

5'-0"

A1          C1

5'-0"

ROOF
LINE

A          C

(84)

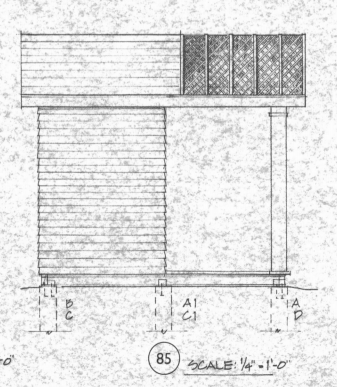

B
C          A1
C1          A
D

(85)   SCALE: 1/4" = 1'-0"

SCALE: 1/4" = 1'-0"

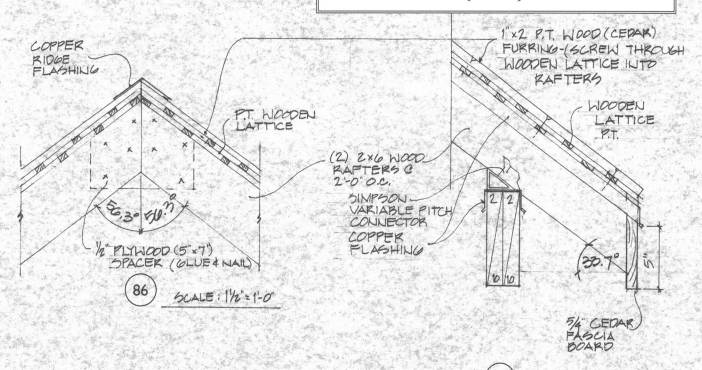

COPPER RIDGE FLASHING

P.T. WOODEN LATTICE

56.3° 56.?°

½" PLYWOOD (5"×7") SPACER (GLUE & NAIL)

86    SCALE: 1½" = 1'-0"

1"×2 P.T. WOOD (CEDAR) FURRING-(SCREW THROUGH WOODEN LATTICE INTO RAFTERS

WOODEN LATTICE P.T.

(2) 2×6 WOOD RAFTERS @ 2'-0" O.C.

SIMPSON VARIABLE PITCH CONNECTOR

COPPER FLASHING

2  2

10  10

33.7°

5"

5/4" CEDAR FASCIA BOARD

87    SCALE: 1½" = 1'-0"

A          C

88    SCALE: ¼" = 1'-0"

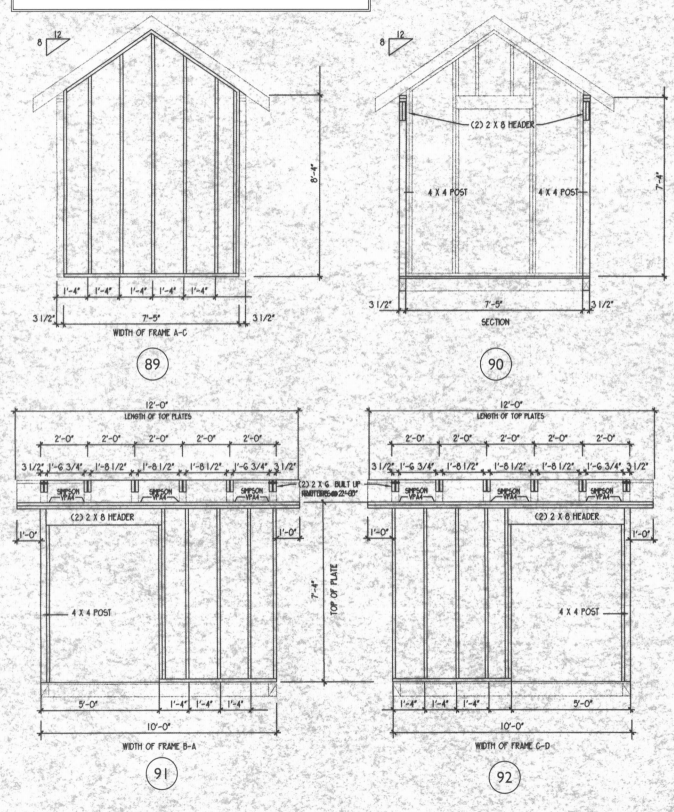

8 [12]

8'-4"

1'-4" 1'-4" 1'-4" 1'-4" 1'-4"

3 1/2"          7'-5"          3 1/2"

WIDTH OF FRAME A-C

89

8 [12]

(2) 2 X 8 HEADER

4 X 4 POST          4 X 4 POST

7'-4"

3 1/2"          7'-5"          3 1/2"

SECTION

90

12'-0"

LENGTH OF TOP PLATES

2'-0"     2'-0"     2'-0"     2'-0"     2'-0"

3 1/2" 1'-6 3/4" 1'-8 1/2" 1'-8 1/2" 1'-8 1/2" 1'-6 3/4" 3 1/2"

SIMPSON VPA4     SIMPSON VPA4     SIMPSON VPA4

(2) 2 X 6 BUILT UP

(2) 2 X 8 HEADER

1'-0"                    1'-0"

4 X 4 POST

5'-0"     1'-4" 1'-4" 1'-4"

10'-0"

WIDTH OF FRAME B-A

91

12'-0"

LENGTH OF TOP PLATES

2'-0"     2'-0"     2'-0"     2'-0"     2'-0"

3 1/2" 1'-6 3/4" 1'-8 1/2" 1'-8 1/2" 1'-8 1/2" 1'-6 3/4" 3 1/2"

SIMPSON VPA4     SIMPSON VPA4     SIMPSON VPA4

(2) 2 X 8 HEADER

TOP OF PLATE

7'-4"

1'-0"                    1'-0"

4 X 4 POST

1'-4" 1'-4" 1'-4"     5'-0"

10'-0"

WIDTH OF FRAME C-D

92

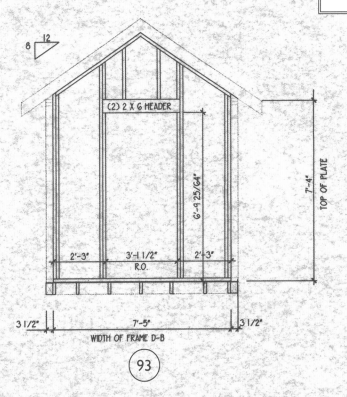

8 | 12

(2) 2 X 6 HEADER

6'-9 25/64"

TOP OF PLATE

7'-4"

2'-3"    3'-11/2"    2'-3"
R.O.

3 1/2"    7'-5"    3 1/2"

WIDTH OF FRAME D-B

93

## ADDITIONAL TOOLS REQUIRED

None

## ADDITIONAL MATERIALS AND SUPPLIES REQUIRED

| DESCRIPTION | QTY. | MATERIAL | DIMENSIONS |
|---|---|---|---|
| Roofing | 1 sq. | standard-width cedar shingles | 16" long |
| | 2 | copper drip | 12' long |
| | 1 | copper ridge flashing | 12' long |
| Canopy | 3 | prefabricated lattice | 4' x 8' |
| Siding | 275 sq.ft. | cedar clapboards | 5½" x 10' |
| Posts | 2 | pressure-treated 4 x 4s | 8' long |
| Door | 1 | ½" CDX plywood | 4' x 8' |
| | 6 | tongue-and-groove cedar | 6" x 8' |

12
8

OPPOSITE
HAND

D
A
(94)
B
C

A1
C1
(95)

OPP
HAND

B
D

8'-0"

A1
10'-0"
C1

ROOF
LINE

A
C
(96) SCALE: 1/4" = 1'-0"

C
C1
D
(97) SCALE: 1/4" = 1'-0"

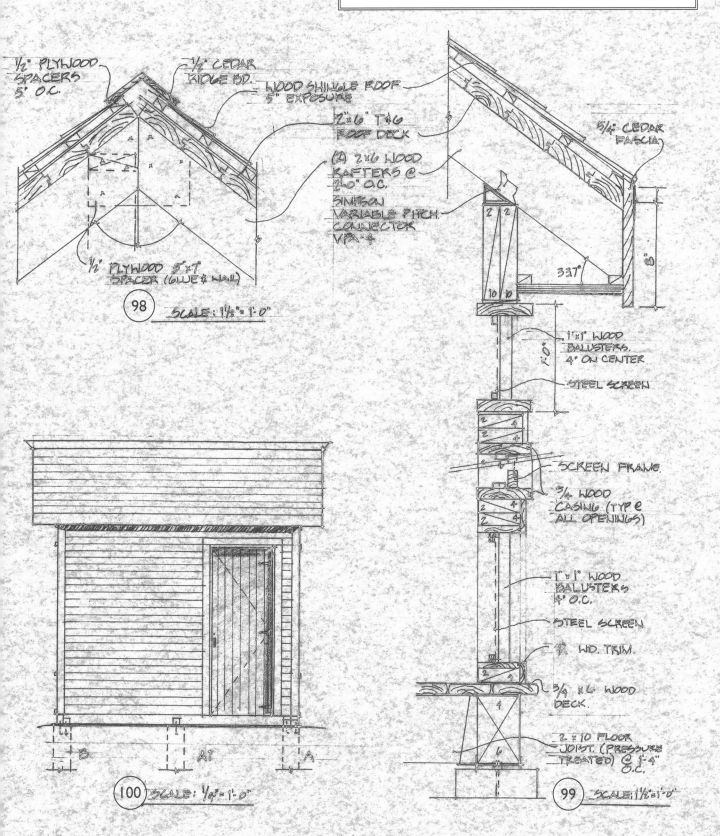

½" PLYWOOD
SPACERS
5" O.C.

½" CEDAR
RIDGE BD.

WOOD SHINGLE ROOF
5" EXPOSURE

2"×6" T&G
ROOF DECK

(2) 2×6 WOOD
RAFTERS @
24" O.C.

SIMPSON
VARIABLE PITCH
CONNECTOR
VPA-4

5/4" CEDAR
FASCIA

½" PLYWOOD 5"×7"
SPACER (GLUE & NAIL)

33°

1"×1" WOOD
BALUSTERS,
4" ON CENTER

STEEL SCREEN

SCREEN FRAME.

3/4 WOOD
CASING (TYP @
ALL OPENINGS)

1"×1" WOOD
BALUSTERS
4" O.C.

STEEL SCREEN

1" WD. TRIM.

3/4 ×6 WOOD
DECK.

2 ×10 FLOOR
JOIST. (PRESSURE
TREATED) @ 1'-4"
O.C.

(98)  SCALE: 1½" = 1'-0"

(100)  SCALE: ¼" = 1'-0"

(99)  SCALE: 1½" = 1'-0"

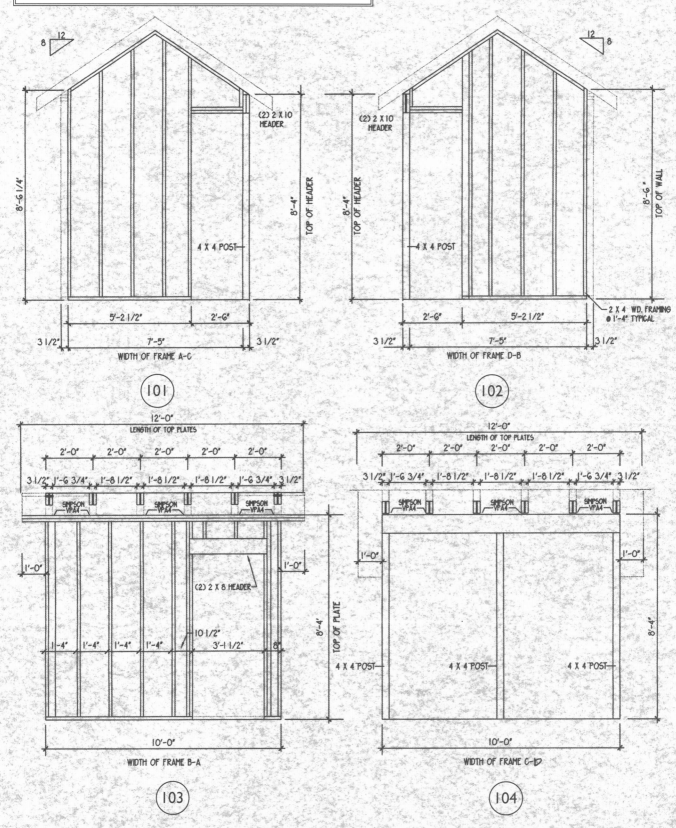

8 / 12

(2) 2 X 10 HEADER

4 X 4 POST

8'-6 1/4"

8'-4" TOP OF HEADER

3 1/2"    5'-2 1/2"    2'-6"    3 1/2"

7'-5"

WIDTH OF FRAME A-C

101

12 / 8

(2) 2 X 10 HEADER

4 X 4 POST

8'-4" TOP OF HEADER

8'-6" TOP OF WALL

3 1/2"    2'-6"    5'-2 1/2"    3 1/2"

7'-5"

2 X 4 WD. FRAMING @ 1'-4" TYPICAL

WIDTH OF FRAME D-B

102

12'-0"

LENGTH OF TOP PLATES

2'-0"    2'-0"    2'-0"    2'-0"    2'-0"

3 1/2"  1'-6 3/4"  1'-8 1/2"  1'-8 1/2"  1'-8 1/2"  1'-6 3/4"  3 1/2"

SIMPSON VPA4    SIMPSON VPA4    SIMPSON VPA4

1'-0"    1'-0"

(2) 2 X 8 HEADER

10 1/2"

1'-4"  1'-4"  1'-4"  1'-4"    3'-11 1/2"    8"

8'-4" TOP OF PLATE

10'-0"

WIDTH OF FRAME B-A

103

12'-0"

LENGTH OF TOP PLATES

2'-0"    2'-0"    2'-0"    2'-0"    2'-0"

3 1/2"  1'-6 3/4"  1'-8 1/2"  1'-8 1/2"  1'-8 1/2"  1'-6 3/4"  3 1/2"

SIMPSON VPA4    SIMPSON VPA4    SIMPSON VPA4

1'-0"    1'-0"

4 X 4 POST    4 X 4 POST    4 X 4 POST

8'-4"

10'-0"

WIDTH OF FRAME C-D

104

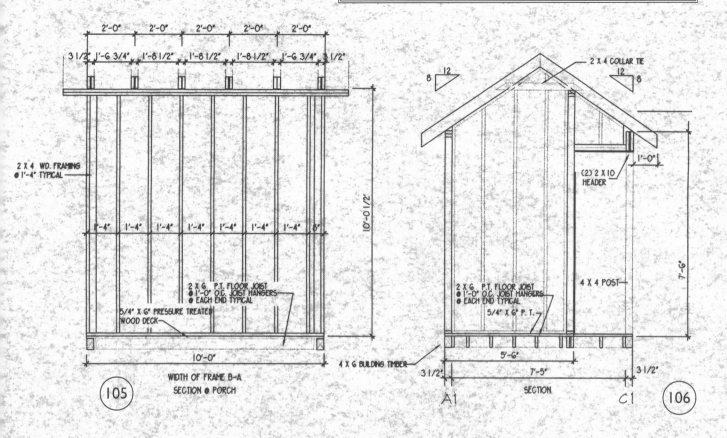

**105** WIDTH OF FRAME B-A
SECTION @ PORCH

**106** SECTION

## ADDITIONAL TOOLS REQUIRED

None

## ADDITIONAL SUPPLIES AND MATERIALS REQUIRED

| DESCRIPTION | QTY. | MATERIAL | DIMENSIONS |
|---|---|---|---|
| Roofing | 2 sq. | standard-width cedar shingles | 16"long |
| | 2 | copper drip | 12' long |
| (Ridge Cap) | 2 | cedar 1 x 6s | 12' long |
| Siding | 310 sq. ft | clapboards | 5½" x 10' |
| Frames | 9 | cedar 1 x 2s | 10' long |
| Casing | 5 | 5/4" x 4" cedar | 10' long |
| Balustrade | 10 | cedar 1 x 1s | 8' long |
| Doors | 3 | ½" CDX plywood | 4' x 8' |
| | 14 | tongue-and-groove cedar | 6" x 8' |

# MINIATURE GREEK REVIVAL LODGE
## (GR-4)

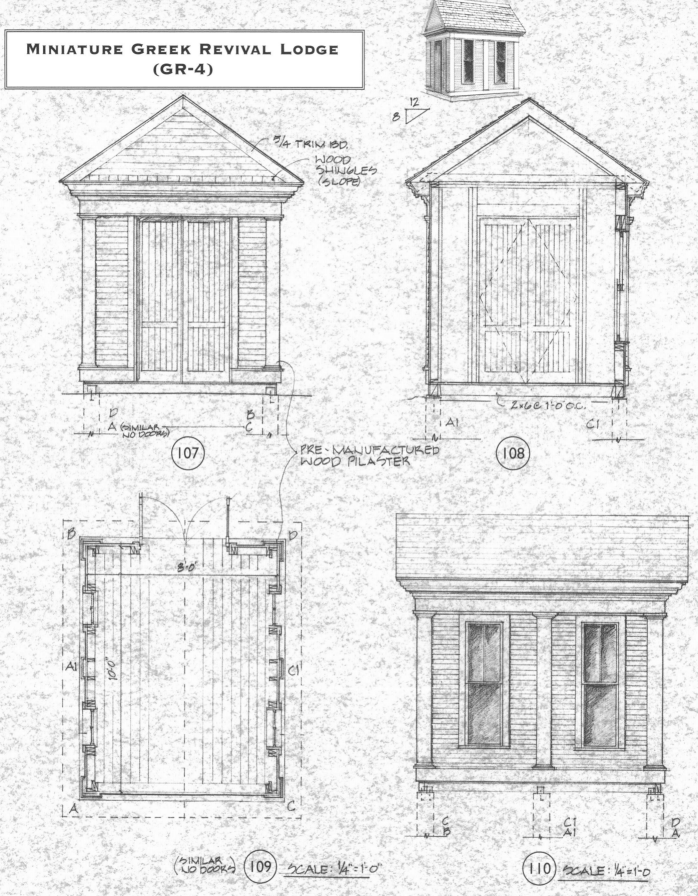

5/4 TRIM BD.

WOOD SHINGLES (SLOPE)

12
8

D    A (SIMILAR NO DOORS)    B
C

107

PRE-MANUFACTURED WOOD PILASTER

2×6 @ 1'-0" O.C.

A1    C1

108

B    3'-0"    D

A1    10'-0"    C1

A    C

(SIMILAR NO DOORS)    109    SCALE: 1/4"=1'-0"

C    C1    D
B    A1    A

110    SCALE: 1/4"=1'-0

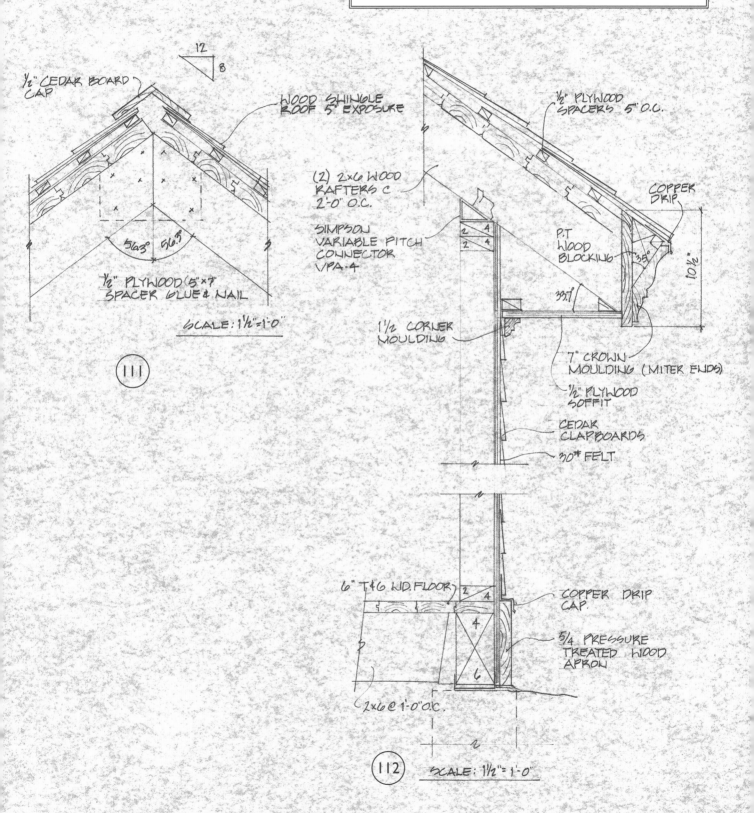

12 / 8

½" CEDAR BOARD CAP

WOOD SHINGLE ROOF 5" EXPOSURE

½" PLYWOOD SPACERS 5" O.C.

COPPER DRIP

56.3° 56.5°

(2) 2×6 WOOD RAFTERS @ 2'-0" O.C.

SIMPSON VARIABLE PITCH CONNECTOR VPA-4

P.T WOOD BLOCKING

35°

10½"

½" PLYWOOD (5"×7") SPACER GLUE & NAIL

33.1°

SCALE: 1½"=1'-0"

⟨111⟩

1½ CORNER MOULDING

7" CROWN MOULDING (MITER ENDS)

½" PLYWOOD SOFFIT

CEDAR CLAPBOARDS

30# FELT

6" T&G WD. FLOOR

COPPER DRIP CAP.

5/4 PRESSURE TREATED WOOD APRON

2×6 @ 1'-0" O.C.

⟨112⟩ SCALE: 1½"=1'-0"

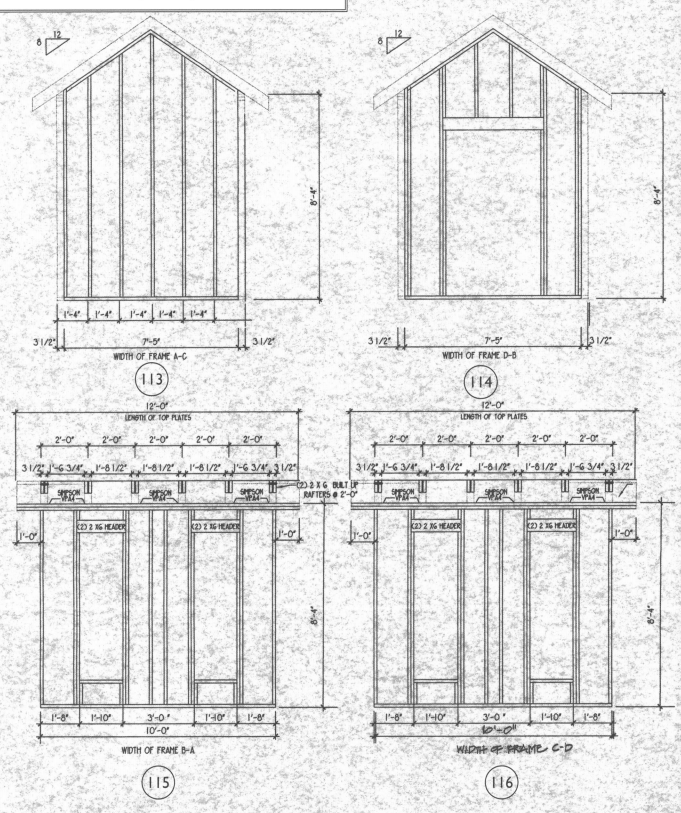

8 12

8'-4"

1'-4" 1'-4" 1'-4" 1'-4" 1'-4"

3 1/2"          7'-5"          3 1/2"

WIDTH OF FRAME A-C

113

8 12

8'-4"

3 1/2"          7'-5"          3 1/2"

WIDTH OF FRAME D-B

114

12'-0"
LENGTH OF TOP PLATES

2'-0"    2'-0"    2'-0"    2'-0"    2'-0"

3 1/2" 1'-6 3/4" 1'-8 1/2" 1'-8 1/2" 1'-8 1/2" 1'-6 3/4" 3 1/2"

SIMPSON VPA4    SIMPSON VPA4    SIMPSON VPA4

(2) 2 X 6 BUILT UP
RAFTERS @ 2'-0"

1'-0"   (2) 2 X6 HEADER    (2) 2 X6 HEADER   1'-0"

8'-4"

1'-8"   1'-10"   3'-0"   1'-10"   1'-8"
10'-0"

WIDTH OF FRAME B-A

115

12'-0"
LENGTH OF TOP PLATES

2'-0"    2'-0"    2'-0"    2'-0"    2'-0"

3 1/2" 1'-6 3/4" 1'-8 1/2" 1'-8 1/2" 1'-8 1/2" 1'-6 3/4" 3 1/2"

SIMPSON VPA4    SIMPSON VPA4    SIMPSON VPA4

1'-0"   (2) 2 X6 HEADER    (2) 2 X6 HEADER   1'-0"

8'-4"

1'-8"   1'-10"   3'-0"   1'-10"   1'-8"
10'-0"

WIDTH OF FRAME C-D

116

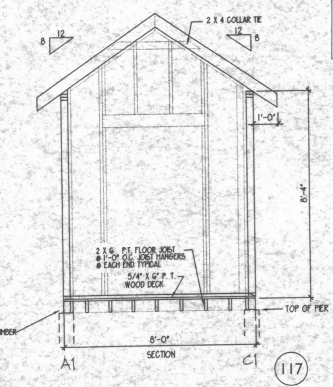

2 X 4 COLLAR TIE

8 | 12          12 | 8

1'-0"

8'-4"

2 X 6 P.T. FLOOR JOIST
@ 1'-0" O.C. JOIST HANGERS
@ EACH END TYPICAL

5/4" X 6" P.T.
WOOD DECK

TOP OF PIER

TIMBER

8'-0"

SECTION

A1          C1          117

# MINIATURE GREEK REVIVAL LODGE (GR-4)

## ADDITIONAL TOOLS REQUIRED

Power Miter Box

Nail Punch

## ADDITIONAL SUPPLIES AND MATERIALS

| DESCRIPTION | QTY. | MATERIAL | DIMENSIONS |
|---|---|---|---|
| Roofing | 2 sq. | standard-width cedar shingles | 16" long |
| | 2 | copper drip | 12' long |
| (Ridge Cap) | 2 | cedar 1 x 6s | 12' long |
| Siding | 250 sq. ft. | cedar clapboards | 5½" x 10' |
| Side Walls | 3 | copper drip | 12' long |
| Posts | 4 | pre-manufactured corner pilasters | 8" x 6'4" |
| | 2 | pre-manufactured pilasters | 8" x 6'4" |
| Wood Apron | 2 | 5/4" x 6" cedar | 12' long |
| | 2 | 5/4" x 6" cedar | 8' long |
| Doors | 2 | ½" CDX plywood | 4' x 8' |
| Windows | 4 | pre-manufactured single-hung wood windows | 1' 9½" x 5'11¾" |
| Moulding | 2 | 7" crown moulding | 10' long |
| | 2 | 7" crown moulding | 12' long |
| | 2 | 1½" corner moulding | 10' long |

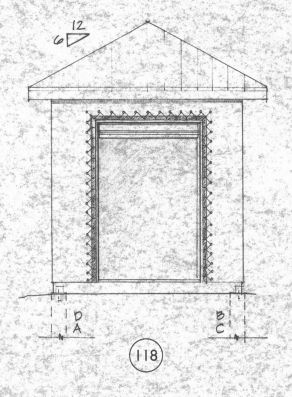

12 / 6

(118)

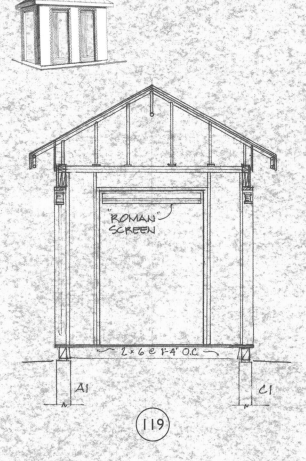

"ROMAN" SCREEN

2×6 @ 1'-4" O.C.

A1

C1

(119)

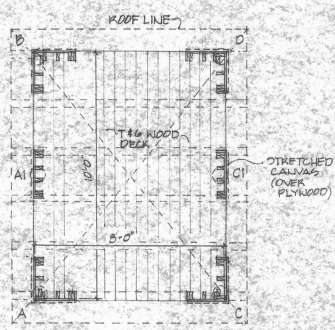

ROOF LINE

B

D

T&G WOOD DECK

10'-0"

A1

C1

8'-0"

A

C

STRETCHED CANVAS (OVER PLYWOOD)

(120) SCALE: 1/4"=1'-0"

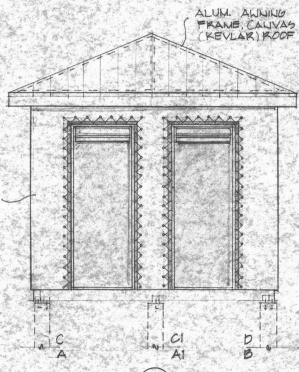

ALUM. AWNING FRAME. CANVAS (KEVLAR) ROOF

C / A

C1 / A1

D / B

(121) SCALE: 1/4"=1'-0"

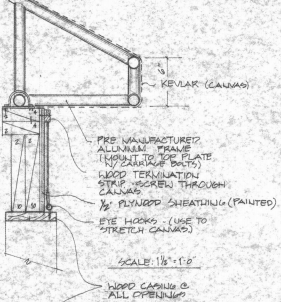

KEVLAR (CANVAS)

PRE-MANUFACTURED ALUMINUM FRAME (MOUNT TO TOP PLATE W/ CARRIAGE BOLTS)

WOOD TERMINATION STRIP - SCREW THROUGH CANVAS.

½" PLYWOOD SHEATHING (PAINTED)

EYE HOOKS - (USE TO STRETCH CANVAS.)

SCALE: 1½" = 1'-0"

WOOD CASING @ ALL OPENINGS

(122)

EYE HOOKS @ 4" O.C. (SCREW INTO WOOD CASING) (EPOXY COATED)

CANVAS (KEVLAR)

BRASS GROMMITS

ELASTIC CHORD

OPENING

4x6 BUILDING TIMBER

(123)

SCALE: 1½" = 1'-0"

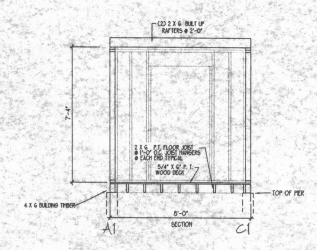

(2) 2 X 6 BUILT UP RAFTERS @ 2'-0"

7'-4"

2 X 6 P.T. FLOOR JOIST @ 1'-0" O.C. JOIST HANGERS @ EACH END TYPICAL

5/4" X 6" P.T. WOOD DECK

4 X 6 BUILDING TIMBER

TOP OF PIER

8'-0"

A1      SECTION      C1

(124)

## ADDITIONAL TOOLS REQUIRED

Grommit Tool (to install metal fasteners for canvas)

## ADDITIONAL SUPPLIES AND MATERIALS REQUIRED

| DESCRIPTION | QTY. | MATERIAL | DIMENSIONS |
|---|---|---|---|
| Roofing | 1 | pre-manufactured aluminum frame and canvas roof with manufacturer's fasteners | 10' x 12' |
| Siding | 325 sq. ft. canvas | | |
| Casing | 11 | 5/4" x 6" cedar | 8' long |
| Openings | 6 | custom wood-slat and canvas | |
| Roman screens | | | |
| Fasteners | 300 | brass grommits | ¼" diameter |
| (for canvas) | 300 | epoxy-coated eye hooks | ½" diameter |
| | 200 ft. | elastic cord | |

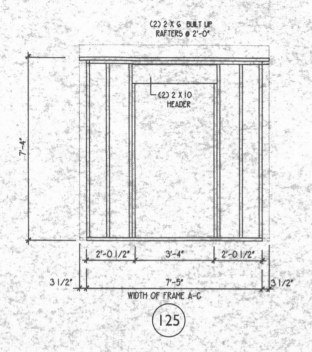

(2) 2 X 6 BUILT UP
RAFTERS @ 2'-0"

(2) 2 X 10
HEADER

7'-4"

2'-0 1/2"  3'-4"  2'-0 1/2"

3 1/2"  7'-5"  3 1/2"

WIDTH OF FRAME A-C

(125)

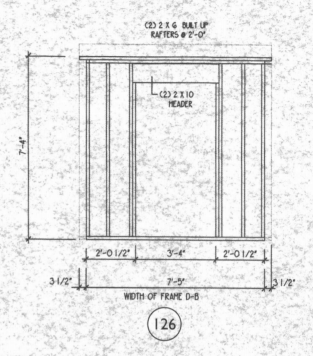

(2) 2 X 6  BUILT UP
RAFTERS @ 2'-0"

(2) 2 X 10
HEADER

7'-4"

2'-0 1/2"  3'-4"  2'-0 1/2"

3 1/2"  7'-5"  3 1/2"

WIDTH OF FRAME D-B

(126)

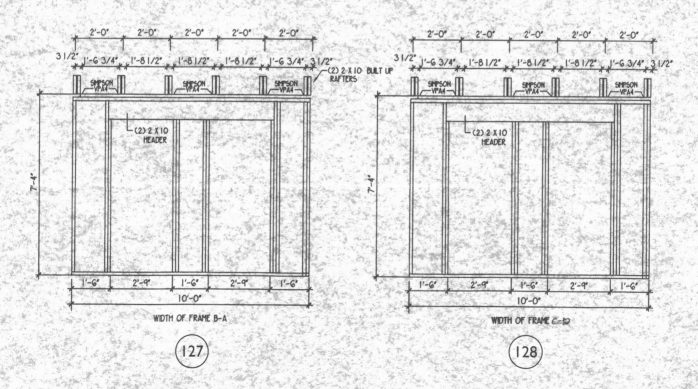

2'-0"  2'-0"  2'-0"  2'-0"  2'-0"

3 1/2"  1'-6 3/4"  1'-8 1/2"  1'-8 1/2"  1'-8 1/2"  1'-6 3/4"  3 1/2"

SIMPSON VPA4  SIMPSON VPA4  SIMPSON VPA4  (2) 2 X 10 BUILT UP RAFTERS

(2) 2 X 10
HEADER

7'-4"

1'-6"  2'-9"  1'-6"  2'-9"  1'-6"

10'-0"

WIDTH OF FRAME B-A

(127)

2'-0"  2'-0"  2'-0"  2'-0"  2'-0"

3 1/2"  1'-6 3/4"  1'-8 1/2"  1'-8 1/2"  1'-8 1/2"  1'-6 3/4"  3 1/2"

SIMPSON VPA4  SIMPSON VPA4  SIMPSON VPA4

(2) 2 X 10
HEADER

7'-4"

1'-6"  2'-9"  1'-6"  2'-9"  1'-6"

10'-0"

WIDTH OF FRAME C-D

(128)

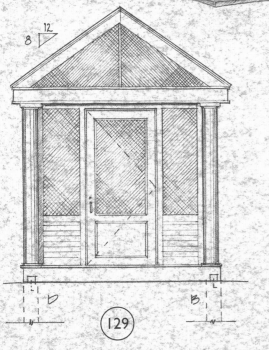

8 12
8

129

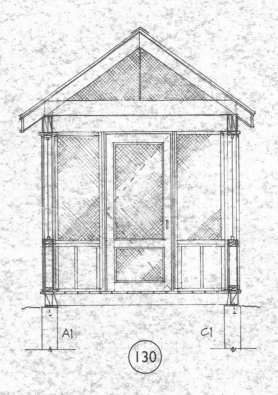

A1    C1

130

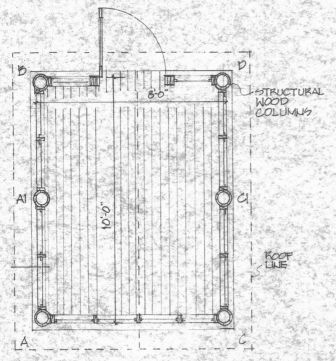

B                        D

8'-0"

STRUCTURAL
WOOD
COLUMNS

A1                        C1

10'-0"

ROOF
LINE

A                        C

131    SCALE: 1/4" = 1'-0"

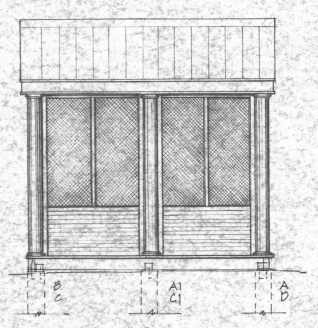

B        A1        A
C        C1        D

132    SCALE: 1/4" = 1'-0"

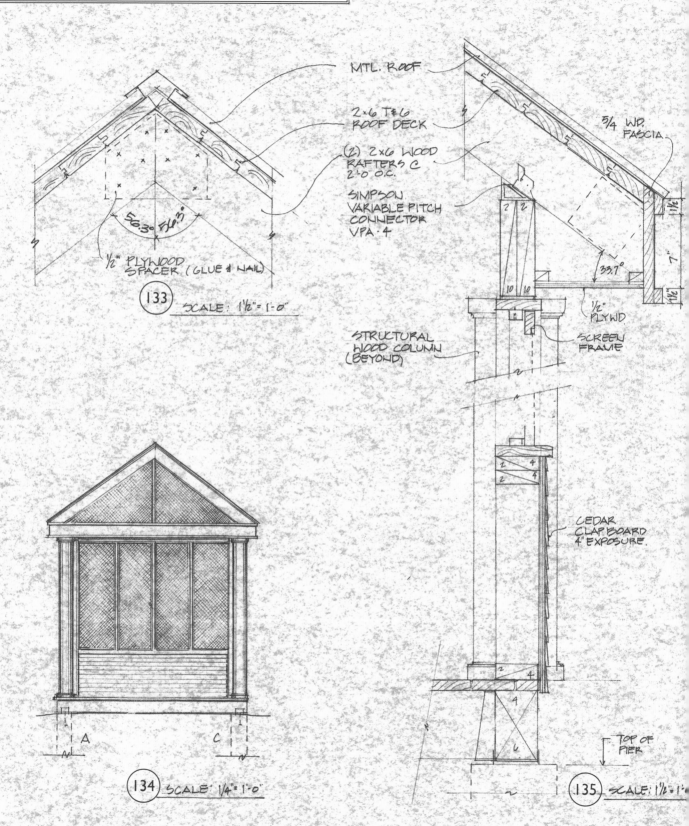

MTL. ROOF

2×6 T&G
ROOF DECK

(2) 2×6 WOOD
RAFTERS C
2'-0 O.C.

SIMPSON
VARIABLE PITCH
CONNECTOR
VPA-4

5/4 WD.
FASCIA

33.7°

1/2" PLYWD.

SCREEN
FRAME

½" PLYWOOD
SPACER (GLUE & NAIL)

⑬ SCALE: 1½" = 1'-0"

STRUCTURAL
WOOD COLUMN
(BEYOND)

CEDAR
CLAPBOARD
4" EXPOSURE.

A          C

TOP OF
PIER

⑭ SCALE: ¼" = 1'-0"

⑮ SCALE: 1½" = 1'-0"

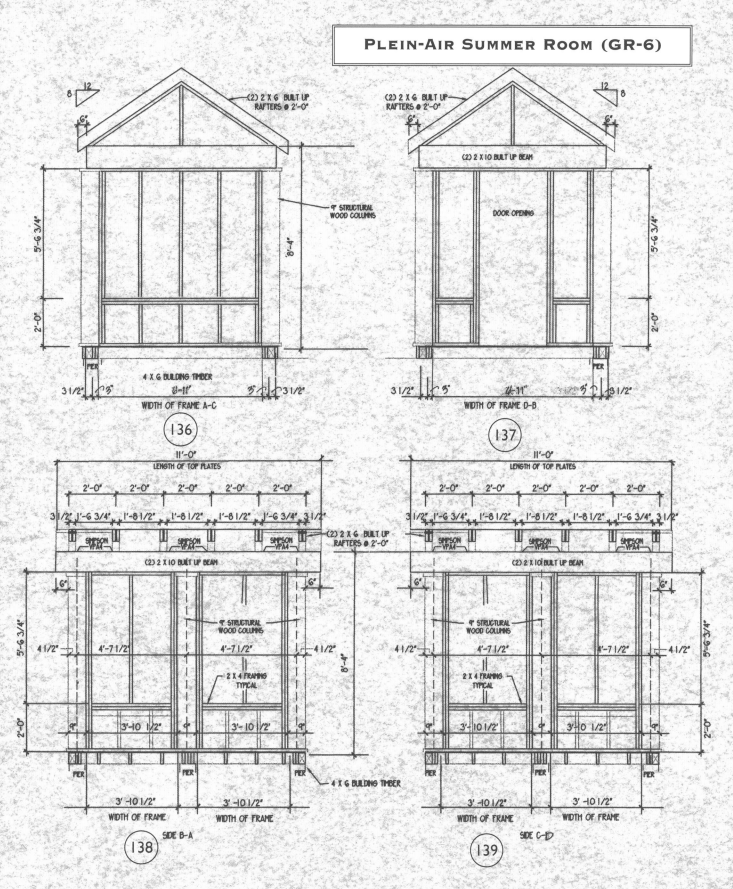

8 / 12

6"

(2) 2 X 6 BUILT UP
RAFTERS @ 2'-0"

9" STRUCTURAL
WOOD COLUMNS

5'-6 3/4"

8'-4"

2'-0"

PIER

4 X 6 BUILDING TIMBER

3 1/2"   3"   8'-11"   5"   3 1/2"

WIDTH OF FRAME A-C

136

12 / 8

6"

(2) 2 X 6 BUILT UP
RAFTERS @ 2'-0"

(2) 2 X 10 BUILT UP BEAM

DOOR OPENING

5'-6 3/4"

2'-0"

PIER

3 1/2"   5"   8'-11"   5"   3 1/2"

WIDTH OF FRAME D-B

137

11'-0"
LENGTH OF TOP PLATES

2'-0"   2'-0"   2'-0"   2'-0"   2'-0"

3 1/2"  1'-6 3/4"  1'-8 1/2"  1'-8 1/2"  1'-8 1/2"  1'-6 3/4"  3 1/2"

SIMPSON
VPA4

SIMPSON
VPA4

SIMPSON
VPA4

(2) 2 X 6 BUILT UP
RAFTERS @ 2'-0"

(2) 2 X 10 BUILT UP BEAM

6"   6"

9" STRUCTURAL
WOOD COLUMNS

5'-6 3/4"

8'-4"

4 1/2"   4'-7 1/2"   4'-7 1/2"   4 1/2"

2 X 4 FRAMING
TYPICAL

2'-0"

9"   3'-10 1/2"   3'-10 1/2"   9"

PIER   PIER   PIER

4 X 6 BUILDING TIMBER

3'-10 1/2"   3'-10 1/2"

WIDTH OF FRAME   WIDTH OF FRAME

138   SIDE B-A

11'-0"
LENGTH OF TOP PLATES

2'-0"   2'-0"   2'-0"   2'-0"   2'-0"

3 1/2"  1'-6 3/4"  1'-8 1/2"  1'-8 1/2"  1'-8 1/2"  1'-6 3/4"  3 1/2"

SIMPSON
VPA4

SIMPSON
VPA4

SIMPSON
VPA4

(2) 2 X 10 BUILT UP BEAM

6"   6"

9" STRUCTURAL
WOOD COLUMNS

5'-6 3/4"

8'-4"

4 1/2"   4'-7 1/2"   4'-7 1/2"   4 1/2"

2 X 4 FRAMING
TYPICAL

2'-0"

9"   3'-10 1/2"   3'-10 1/2"   9"

PIER   PIER   PIER

3'-10 1/2"   3'-10 1/2"

WIDTH OF FRAME   WIDTH OF FRAME

139   SIDE C-D

# PLEIN-AIR SUMMER ROOM (GR-6)

## ADDITIONAL TOOLS REQUIRED

Staple Gun

Power Miter Box

Nail Punch

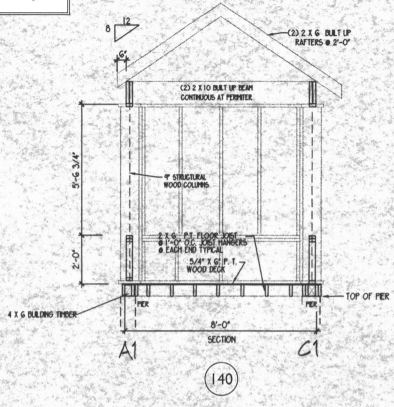

## ADDITIONAL SUPPLIES AND MATERIALS REQUIRED

| DESCRIPTION | QTY. | MATERIAL | DIMENSIONS |
|---|---|---|---|
| Roofing | 12 sheets | pre-manufactured metal roofing | 2' x 6' |
| (Ridge cap) | 1 | pre-manufactured metal ridge cap | 11' long |
| Siding | 48 sq. ft. | cedar clapboards | 5½"x 10' |
| Frames | 24 cedar | 1 x 2s | 10'long |
| | 6 | 5/4" x 4" cedar | 10' long |
| Sills | 4 | 5/4" x 6" cedar | 8' long |
| Door | 1 | prefabricated screened wood door | 3' x 6' 8" |
| Window | 110 ft. | 36" metal screen | 12' long |
| Posts | 6 | pre-manufactured wood columns | 9" diameter |

# TINY STONE COTTAGE (GR-7)

12
8

A
D

C
B

(141)

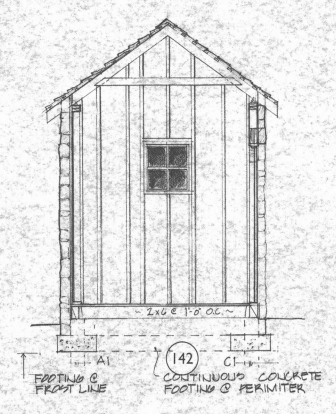

~ 2x6 @ 1'-0" O.C. ~

A1                    C1

(142)

FOOTING @
FROST LINE

CONTINUOUS CONCRETE
FOOTING @ PERIMITER

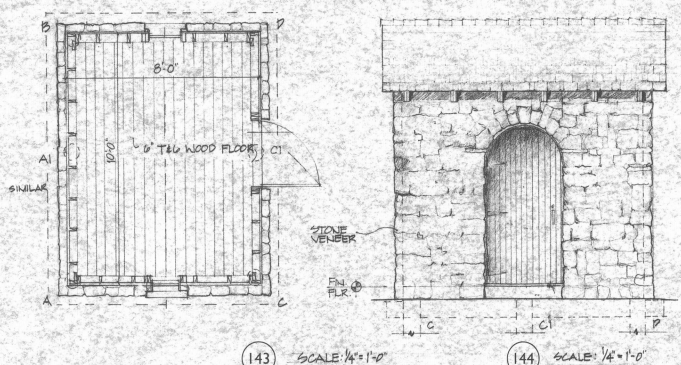

B                              D

8'-0"

10'-0"

A1

SIMILAR

6" T&G WOOD FLOOR          C1

A                              C

STONE
VENEER

FIN.
FLR. ⊕

C              C1            P

(143)  SCALE: 1/4"=1'-0"          (144)  SCALE: 1/4"=1'-0"

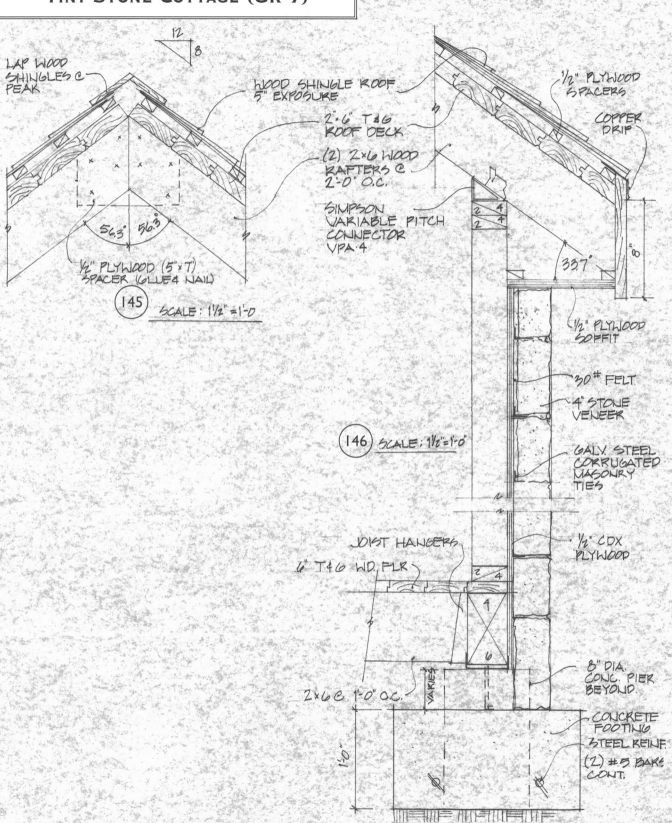

LAP WOOD
SHINGLES @
PEAK

12
8

WOOD SHINGLE ROOF
5" EXPOSURE

2"×6" T&G
ROOF DECK

(2) 2×6 WOOD
RAFTERS @
2'-0" O.C.

½" PLYWOOD
SPACERS

COPPER
DRIP

56.3°   56.3°

½" PLYWOOD (5"×7")
SPACER (GLUE& NAIL)

SIMPSON
VARIABLE PITCH
CONNECTOR
VPA·4

33.7°

8"

145   SCALE : 1½" = 1'-0

2   4
2   4

½" PLYWOOD
SOFFIT

30# FELT

4" STONE
VENEER

146   SCALE : 1½" = 1'-0

GALV. STEEL
CORRUGATED
MASONRY
TIES

JOIST HANGERS

6" T&G WD. FLR.

2   4

½" CDX
PLYWOOD

4

6

8" DIA.
CONC. PIER
BEYOND.

CONCRETE
FOOTING
STEEL REINF

2×6 @ 1'-0" O.C.

VARIES

1'-0"

(2) #5 BARS
CONT.

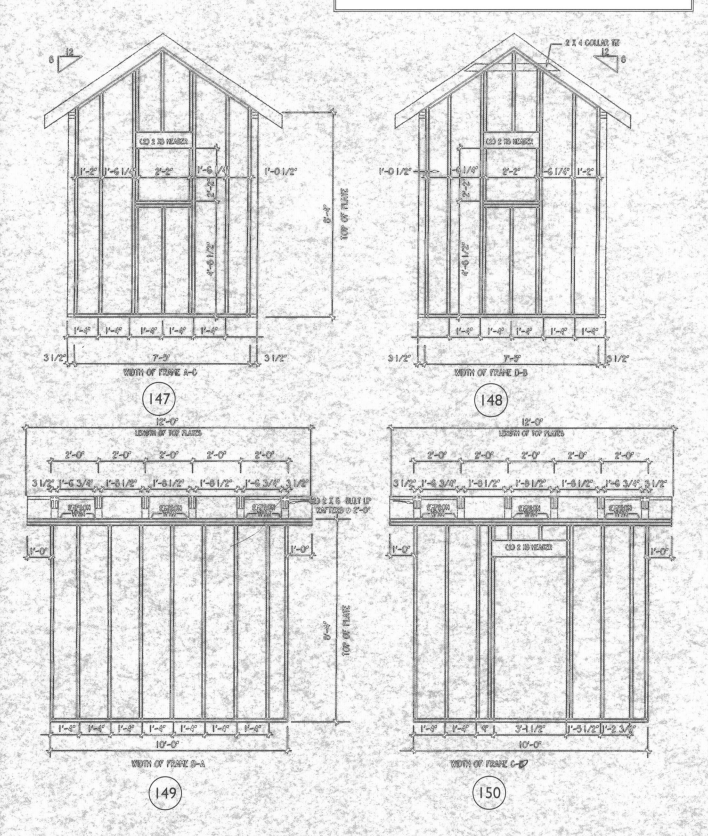

2 X 4 COLLAR TIE

8 | 12

12 | 8

(2) 2 X8 HEADER

1'-2"  1'-6 1/4"  2'-2"  1'-6 1/4"  1'-0 1/2"

2'-2"

4'-6 1/2"

8'-0"
TOP OF PLATE

1'-4"  1'-4"  1'-4"  1'-4"  1'-4"

3 1/2"  7'-5"  3 1/2"

WIDTH OF FRAME A-C

(147)

1'-0 1/2"  1'-6 1/4"  2'-2"  1'-6 1/4"  1'-2"

2'-2"

4'-6 1/2"

1'-4"  1'-4"  1'-4"  1'-4"  1'-4"

3 1/2"  7'-5"  3 1/2"

WIDTH OF FRAME D-B

(148)

12'-0"
LENGTH OF TOP PLATES

2'-0"  2'-0"  2'-0"  2'-0"  2'-0"

3 1/2"  1'-6 3/4"  1'-8 1/2"  1'-8 1/2"  1'-8 1/2"  1'-6 3/4"  3 1/2"

SIMPSON H2.5A

(2) 2 X 6 BUILT UP
RAFTERS @ 2'-0"

1'-0"  1'-0"

8'-0"
TOP OF PLATE

1'-4"  1'-4"  1'-4"  1'-4"  1'-4"  1'-4"  1'-4"

10'-0"

WIDTH OF FRAME B-A

(149)

12'-0"
LENGTH OF TOP PLATES

2'-0"  2'-0"  2'-0"  2'-0"  2'-0"

3 1/2"  1'-6 3/4"  1'-8 1/2"  1'-8 1/2"  1'-8 1/2"  1'-6 3/4"  3 1/2"

SIMPSON H2.5A

1'-0"  1'-0"

(2) 2 X8 HEADER

1'-4"  1'-4"  4"  3'-1 1/2"  1'-5 1/2"  1'-2 3/4"

10'-0"

WIDTH OF FRAME C-D

(150)

# TINY STONE COTTAGE (GR-7)

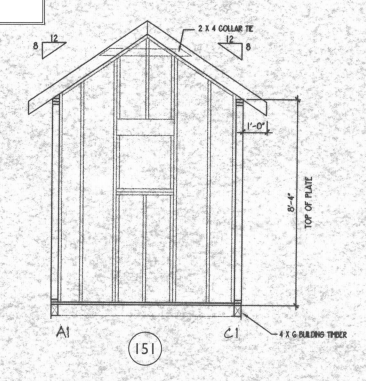

## ADDITIONAL TOOLS REQUIRED

Nail Punch

Trowel

## ADDITIONAL SUPPLIES AND MATERIALS REQUIRED:

| DESCRIPTION | QTY. | MATERIAL | DIMENSIONS |
|---|---|---|---|
| Roofing | 2 sq. | standard-width cedar shingles | 16"-long |
| | 2 | copper drip | 12'-long |
| Siding | 350 sq. ft. | 4"-wide veneer stone | variable |
| Door | 1 | ½" CDX plywood | 4' x 8' |
| | 6 | tongue-and-groove cedar | 6" x 8' |
| Windows | 2 | pre-manufactured single-hung wood window | 2'½" x 2'1½" |
| Footings | 4 | #5 steel rebar | 11' long |
| | 4 | #5 steel rebar | 9' long |
| Fasteners | 160 | galvanized metal masonry ties | 8" |
| | 1 | 80-lb bag mason's cement | |
| | 1 box | galvanized metal roof nails | |

# ACKNOWLEDGEMENTS

Many, many thanks to all of the following individuals, organizations, institutions, and businesses for their gracious help and interest in putting together this book.

For allowing us to include their wonderful sheds in this book: (in Asheville, North Carolina, and the surrounding area) Jack and Helga Bean, Dr. Peter and Cathy Wallenborn, Kirk and Gaye Symmes, W.C. Justice, Thomas Rain Crowe, Ivan Prim and Joie Power, Wanda and Harvey Austin, the Cherokee Historical Association, Mountain Gardens, and the Vance Memorial Birthplace; (in Greenville, South Carolina, and the surrounding area) Tom and Jan Vestal (cover), Frank and Micki Gannon, Don and Kay King, Riley Owens, and Pat Schweitzer and Allen Vilcheck; T. Hunter McEaddy (Charleston, South Carolina); Jean Hamel (Fairport, New York); John and Kathleen Holmes (Penngrove, California); Bob Comings and the Nada Farm Museum of Archetypes (Willits, California); James Stageberg (Minneapolis, Minnesota); B.J. Wyckoff (Beaver Island, Michigan); Joszsef Balogh (Pribenik, Hungary; photo by Richard Budd); Bob and Cathy Collier (Clinton, Ohio); (in Hudson, Ohio) Pat and Debra Michael, Mercy Sorgi, Valerie Strong, Charlie and April Walton, and Ramona Kerrigan; Stan Hywet Hall and Gardens (Akron, Ohio); the Kingswood Center (Mansfield, Ohio); Hiram College (Hiram, Ohio); San Antonio Botanical Gardens (San Antonio, Texas); Wave Hill Public Gardens (Bronx, New York); Sonnenberg Gardens (Cananaigua, New York); Sol y Sombra (Santa Fe, New Mexico; photo by Reid Callahan); Tucson Botanical Gardens (Tucson, Arizona); Monticello (Charlottesville, Virginia); and Maymont (Richmond, Virginia). (Thanks, too, to all the folks who sent photos of great sheds we were not able to include.)

For contributing photos of the marvelous sheds they design and build: William Cahill (thatched garden sheds), P.O. Box 62054, Cincinnati, Ohio (513-772-4974); Nellie Ahl of Gardensheds, 651 Millcross Road, Lancaster, Pennsylvania; Stephen Pannell of Little Mansions, Ltd., 936 West Baltimore Pike, Kennett Square, Pennsylvania; Tony Nissen of Once Upon A Time, P.O. Box 2321, Blue Jay, California.

For kindly lending their photographs of myriad and wonderful garden sheds and buildings: Sue L'Hommedieu (sheds in Ohio and Virginia); Heather Smith (sheds in Maine); and Lyn Dawson ( Norwegian and other Scandinavian sheds).

For leading us to great sheds and arranging for location photography: Graham Kimak, Dabney Peeples, and all the staff at JDP Design in Easley, South Carolina, and Beverly Hill in Celo, North Carolina.

For lending props: Perri Crutcher of Perri Ltd. Floral Decor Studio in Asheville, North Carolina; Larry and Genevieve Burda of Do It Best Hardware in Mars Hill, North Carolina; Cindy Burda, Chris Rich, Laura Dover Doran, Thom Gaines, Norman Dawson, and Dr. Heather Spencer.

For his great shed designs and renderings, gifts of invaluable information, great attitude, and ability to turn on a dime, Barry Hamel.

For patiently and good-naturedly sharing their building knowldege and expertise, Bill Taylor of Archadeck of Asheville and his construction foreman, Mark Dewberry (special thanks to Mark for maintaining a sense of humor while building our shed under a punishing August sun and stopping to pose for photographs.)

For providing a building site for the Potting Shed, Richard Babb; for bearing with us while we turned her garden space into a construction zone, Ruth Anne Kah; for posing agreeably for photos, Nuisance the cat.

For her phenomenal index, Jackie Flenner.

For her superlative eye, style, and all-around help, Dana Irwin, art director; for her fantastic organization, keen research abilities, and indomitable high spirits, Heather Smith, editorial assistant; for his great photography and flexibility, Richard Babb; for her gorgeous illustrations, Bernie Wolf; for her meticulous reading, Catharine Sutherland, assistant editor; and for cheerfully scanning endless images, Hannes Charen, production assistant.

## METRIC CONVERSIONS

| INCHES | CM | INCHES | CM |
|---|---|---|---|
| 1/8 | 0.3 | 20 | 50.8 |
| 1/4 | 0.6 | 21 | 53.3 |
| 3/8 | 1.0 | 22 | 55.9 |
| 1/2 | 1.3 | 23 | 58.4 |
| 5/8 | 1.6 | 24 | 61.0 |
| 3/4 | 1.9 | 25 | 63.5 |
| 7/8 | 2.2 | 26 | 66.0 |
| 1 | 2.5 | 27 | 68.6 |
| 1 1/4 | 3.2 | 28 | 71.1 |
| 1 1/2 | 3.8 | 29 | 73.7 |
| 1 3/4 | 4.4 | 30 | 76.2 |
| 2 | 5.1 | 31 | 78.7 |
| 2 1/2 | 6.4 | 32 | 81.3 |
| 3 | 7.6 | 33 | 83.8 |
| 3 1/2 | 8.9 | 34 | 86.4 |
| 4 | 10.2 | 35 | 88.9 |
| 4 1/2 | 11.4 | 36 | 91.4 |
| 5 | 12.7 | 37 | 94.0 |
| 6 | 15.2 | 38 | 96.5 |
| 7 | 17.8 | 39 | 99.1 |
| 8 | 20.3 | 40 | 101.6 |
| 9 | 22.9 | 41 | 104.1 |
| 10 | 25.4 | 42 | 106.7 |
| 11 | 27.9 | 43 | 109.2 |
| 12 | 30.5 | 44 | 111.8 |
| 13 | 33.0 | 45 | 114.3 |
| 14 | 35.6 | 46 | 116.8 |
| 15 | 38.1 | 47 | 119.4 |
| 16 | 40.6 | 48 | 121.9 |
| 17 | 43.2 | 49 | 124.5 |
| 18 | 45.7 | 50 | 127.0 |
| 19 | 48.3 | | |

# INDEX